THE CHARISMATIC GIFT OF
PROPHECY

THE CHARISMATIC GIFT OF
PROPHECY

A Reformed Response to Wayne Grudem

Kenneth L. Gentry, Jr., Th.D.

Fountain Inn, SC 29644 USA

"Proclaiming the kingdom of God and teaching those things which concern
the Lord Jesus Christ, with all confidence."
(Acts 28:31)

The Charismatic Gift of Prophecy: A Reformed Response to Wayne Grudem
by Kenneth L. Gentry, Jr., Th.D.

Second Edition Copyright © 1989 by Gentry Family Trust udt April 2, 1999
VICTORIOUS HOPE PUBLISHING publication date: 2011
This book is a reprint of the previously published 1989 Wipf & Stock edition.

Printed in the United States of America

ISBN 978-0-9826206-2-5

All rights reserved. No part of this book may be reproduced in any form or by any means, except for brief quotations for the purpose of review, comment, or scholarship, without written permission from Victorious Hope Publishing.

Victorious Hope Publishing
P.O. Box 1874
Fountain Inn, South Carolina 29644

Website: www.VictoriousHope.com
E-mail: TheologyMail@cs.com

VICTORIOUS HOPE PUBLISHING is committed to producing Christian educational materials for promoting the whole Bible for the whole of life. We are conservative, evangelical, and Reformed and are committed to the doctrinal formulation found in the Westminster Standards.

Dedicated to

Dr. George W. Knight III

Reformed Scholar and Defender of the Faith

Table Of Contents

Introduction i

Part I: Exegetical Questions
1. The Prophetic Line 1
2. Analysis of New Testament Terms .... .13
3. Authority of New Testament Prophets 26
4. Alleged Problem Passages .... .51

Part II: Historical Questions
5. A Survey of Reformed Opinion 75
6. A Survey of Evangelical Opinion 98
7. An Survey of John Calvin's Writings 108

Part III: Ecclesiastical Questions
8. The Westminster Confession of Faith 118
9. The Presbyterian Church in America 124

Part IV: Theological Questions
10. The Problem of the "Open Canon" 131
11. The Problem in the Book of Revelation 136

Conclusion .... .143

Scripture Index 145

Introduction

Our Purpose

The chapters contained in this book were originally drawn up in the context of a particular theological debate among Reformed brethren in the Presbyterian Church in America, a conservative and evangelical Reformed denomination. In my understanding the debate especially concerned four leading questions:

(1) What is the nature of the New Testament "gift of prophecy"?

(2) What was the role of the New Testament "prophet" in Scripture?

(3) May the continuance of the "prophet" and the "gift of prophecy" be expected in the present era?

(4) Do the answers to these questions touch on fundamental issues in regard to the integrity of the Reformed faith?

For the most part, the following chapters were originally formulated as position papers drawn up by the author and in the particular ecclesiastical context mentioned above.[1] In fact, the first edition of the present work was nothing but an inexpensive, limited circulation, bound collection of the papers, which was quickly published by Whitefield Theological Seminary Press in response to the ongoing debate. That limited circulation edition served its purpose in providing a quick, easily accessible response for those interested in the denominational debate to which it responded.

The original collection of papers was developed in response to what the writer believes were ostensibly anti-Reformed, pro-charismatic positions taken by some Reformed brethren during the rather extensive presbytery and de-

---

[1] See Chapter 9 for more details.

nominational debate engaged in 1985-1986. In that the thorny matter revolved around a serious theological issue, rather than personal or procedural matters, the papers published in the first edition were slightly revised to omit critical reference to particular contemporary ministers and their individual positions. It is imperative that neither particular personalities nor personal experiences become a focal — or even a peripheral — consideration in this important question, which regards a *biblico-theological* issue.

It is the deep conviction of the present writer that the questions engaged in that debate, which are still before the broader evangelical and Reformed church today, are of grave significance — both theologically and practically. The gravity of this situation should be apparent within confessionally Reformed churches, as well as within other evangelical circles. Unfortunately, such is not always the case.

The Importance of the Issues

Practically, it is doubtful whether anyone would dispute the fact that the charismatic movement is one of the most vocal, vibrant, and rapidly growing movements within Christianity today. Hence, it is an issue in which those engaged in ecclesiastical labor will eventually face in their ministries, whether on the local (congregational), or the regional (presbyterial), or the national (denominational) levels. Paul does not want us to be "ignorant brethren." The issue *is* before the church and *must* be dealt with appropriately, which means that it must be confronted at the practical level, as well as being analyzed biblically and theologically.

Theologically, the questions explicated in this work relate to certain aspects of charismatic theology and experience which are of serious moment. The seriousness of these questions (as will be shown) is that they necessarily impact our view both of the sufficiency of Scripture and the outworking of redemptive history.[2] These are issues of the first order of magnitude, particularly in our age in which the very reliability of Scripture (among liberal religionists) and the legitimacy of the Christian experience (due to public abuses of trust by certain "evangelical" televangelists) are so widely questioned.

Our Approach

The following chapters are revised and expanded from the earlier edition. The *revision* basically has been along the lines of format and readability; the position and approach remain fundamentally unaltered. The *expansion* of the argument is designed to take into account an excellent counter analysis that recently has been published. That recent work is by respected and capable theologian Dr. Wayne A. Grudem of Trinity Evangelical Divinity School. The title of his work, which is a popularization of his doctoral dissertation, is *The Gift of Prophecy in the New Testament and Today* (1988).

Consequently, we will incorporate interaction with his arguments into our presentation, and will even add additional sections made necessary by his treatment. Because of our restricted size and summary purpose, we will not challenge *every* matter in Grudem's work. Nevertheless, we hope that an adequate response to Grudem is provided herein by our expansion to include some of his more significant arguments. Grudem's careful work contains the best contrary argument available, in our opinion. And it certainly has sterling endorsements from leading evangelical and Reformed theologians, including J. I. Packer, Vern S. Poythress, Charles L. Holman, L. Russ Bush, Stanley Horton, H. Wayne House, and F. F. Bruce.

---

[2] Wayne A. Grudem in his *The Gift of Prophecy In the New Testament and Today* (Westchester, IL: Crossway Books, 1988) disagrees, though, we believe, wrongly.

Our book then, is basically a manual for dealing with certain of the fundamental issues arising in the debate. It is being republished in expanded and updated form in response to a demand evidenced by inquiries to the author. This study manual is presented with the sincere hope that it may shed some additional light on the questions outlined above. Undoubtedly, these questions will continue to arise even in theologically cautious Presbyterian and Reformed circles.

Summary of Our Approach

The studies within are basically of four sorts. The primary study (contained in Part I) is exegetical. It answers the fundamental question: "What saith the Lord?" It elucidates the Biblical teaching regarding the role of the prophet in Scripture (Chapter 1), with particular emphasis on the New Testament prophet (Chapters 2-3). It even engages several of the major alleged problem passages frequently brought forth in the discussion (Chapter 4). This section should be of interest to both Reformed and non-Reformed Christians.

The second class of studies includes those which present illustratively historical matters of Reformed and evangelical precedent. Part II illustrates the historic evangelical position by surveying the statements of a number of noteworthy Reformed (Chapter 5) and evangelical (Chapter 6) scholars. This serves to demonstrate that the present author's own position is in the main stream of evangelical thought. In addition, a special study is given over to a consideration of the confusion regarding statements in John Calvin's writings, for these are often brought forward in Reformed debate over the charismatic question (Chapter 7).

The third class of studies in Part III is directed to consideration of Reformed *ecclesiastical* matters. Chapter 8 provides a brief analysis of the Westminster Standards, which Standards have exercised a considerable influence in Reformed theology in general. Chapter 9 sets forth the Reformed debate as it has been experienced in a particular

Reformed denomination, the author's own ecclesiastical connection, the Presbyterian Church in America.

In Part IV two important theological challenges are met that have arisen in response to the overall position presented in the preceding chapters. These "problems" are those presented to the Church regarding the theoretical possibility of an open canon (Chapter 10) and with the prophets in the Book of Revelation, whose appearance suggest the gift of prophecy continues in the church into the future (Chapter 11).

Thus, the work is a mixture of exegetical, historical, ecclesiastical, and theological argumentation. As such it should speak to a number of issues, despite its relatively small size. Its format, then, provides more of a handbook on the issues, than either a dissertation-like analysis or a popular exposition.

Before closing this Introduction, I would like to thank my good friend, Mr. Bill Boney, for his time and trouble in preparing the Scripture Index for me. Bill is a budding theologian in his own right, and a constant source of encouragement to me.

Part I
EXEGETICAL QUESTIONS

1

The Prophetic Line

Evangelical Christians hold to both the full inspiration and the organic unity of the entire Scriptures. We are convinced that "all Scripture is inspired by God" (2 Tim. 3:16a). Thus, we hold that "every word" in Scripture "proceeds out of the mouth of God" (Matt. 4:8) and that "the Scripture cannot be broken" (John 10:35b). Consequently, regarding the particular question before us, it is important for us to recognize the Old Testament backdrop to the New Testament prophet. Contrary to much contemporary belief and practice, the Old Testament is a part of the canon of Scripture for the Church today.[1]

As a distinctive difference between his view and ours, Grudem disavows any continuity between the Old Testament prophets and New Testament prophets. He sees the express link between the Old and New Testament in this area as solely between the Old Testament prophets and the New Testament *apostles*:

> At first we might expect that New Testament prophets would be like the Old Testament prophets. But when we look through the New Testament itself this does not seem to be case. There is little if any evidence for a group of *prophets* in the New Testament churches who could speak with God's very words (with 'absolute

---

[1] Contra Meredith G. Kline, *The Structure of Biblical Authority* (2nd ed.: Grand Rapids: Wm. B. Eerdmans, 1975); Douglas J. Moo, "The Law of Moses or the Law of Christ" in John S. Feinberg, ed., *Continuity and Discontinuity: Perspectives on the Relationship Between the Old and New Testaments* (Westchester, IL: Crossway Books, 1988), pp. 203-220.

> divine authority' that could not be questioned) and who had the authority to write books of scripture for inclusion in the New Testament.
>
> On the other hand, there is a very prominent group of people in the New Testament who *do* speak with absolute divine authority and who *did* write most of the books of the New Testament. These men are called not 'prophets', however, but 'apostles.' In many ways they are similar to the Old Testament prophets.[2]

Despite his assertion and the evidence he offers for it (which we will challenge later), we do not believe his case is as strong as it might initially appear. The view we believe to be most scriptural may be discerned by tracing the prophetic line in Scripture. The New Testament prophet (and its actualizing gift of prophecy) does not appear out of the blue in the biblical record. New Testament history cannot be understood apart from its Old Testament connection; this is as true for the dispensationalist as it is for the covenantal Christian.

In this regard, it is vital that the *line of continuity* connecting the stream of prophets in the Old Testament be recognized. Even a cursory survey of the Biblical record demonstrates that this line continues through the Old Testament and *into the New Testament*. We will seek summarily to suggest this by reference to four key passages.

Deuteronomy 18:15-22

> I will raise up a prophet from among their countrymen like you, and I will put My words in his mouth, and he shall speak to them all that I command him. And it shall come about that whoever will not listen to My words which he shall speak in My name, I Myself will require it of him. But the prophet who shall speak a word presumptuously in My name which I have not commanded him to speak, or which he shall speak in the name of other gods, that prophet shall die. And you may say in your heart, How shall we know the word which the Lord has not spoken?" When a prophet speaks in the name of the Lord, if the thing does not come about or come true, that is the thing which the Lord has not spoken. The

---

[2] Grudem, *Gift of Prophecy*, p. 25.

prophet has spoken it presumptuously; you shall not be afraid of him.

Deuteronomy 18:15-22 contains a fundamentally important revelation with regard to the *office* of the prophet. Of course, in this passage Christ is presented as *the* Prophet, *par excellence*. The ancient Church fathers rightly recognized the Christocentric nature of this passage, for it is based on the interpretation found in the New Testament record itself (Acts 3:22; 7:37; cp. Matt. 21:11; John 1:25; 6:14; 7:40).

Yet not only is Christ prophesied as the coming Great Prophet, but the very *line* of the prophets here receives its divine establishment, as well — which establishment the fathers were not as prone to see.[3] As Craigie puts it: "The legislation [in Deuteronomy 18] . . . has two levels of significance. Its immediate significance lies in the provision for the continuation of prophecy after the decease of the prophet Moses. But in addition, the passage is in itself prophetic, as the New Testament interpretation makes clear."[4] Thus, this passage is the divine legislation which establishes, authorizes, and legitimates the prophetic institution.[5]

Some have disputed this function of Deuteronomy 18 due to the presence of the singular noun "the prophet." On this basis, they have assumed it must refer only to Christ,

---

[3] See C. F. Keil and F. Delitzsch, *The Pentateuch*, vol. 3 of *Commentary on the Old Testament*, trans. by James Martin (Grand Rapids: Wm. B. Eerdmans, rep. 1975), p. 395.

[4] P. C. Craigie, *The Book of Deuteronomy* (NICOT) (Grand Rapids: Wm. B. Eerdmans, 1976), pp. 262.

[5] In addition to Craigie see also: Roland Kenneth Harrison, *Introduction to the Old Testament with a Comprehensive Review of Old Testament Studies and a Special Supplement on the Apocrypha* (Grand Rapids: Wm. B. Eerdmans, 1969), p. 741. Keil and Delitzsch, Pentateuch, 3:392ff. Geerhardus Vos, *Biblical Theology: Old and New Testaments* (Grand Rapids: Wm. B. Eerdmans, 1948), pp. 118ff, 217-218.

the Great Prophet. While considering this possibility, three interpretive considerations must be borne in mind. (1) The singular noun, "the prophet," is a collective singular indicating the prophets considered as a single, unified group.[6] (2) The verb rendered "will raise up" has a distributive sense, meaning "will raise up from time to time."[7] Thus, the verb idea requires a plurality of prophets, i.e., the prophetic line. (3) Moses makes express reference to the potential appearance of a "false prophet" (Deut. 18:22). This obviously cannot apply to Christ and must therefore indicate a prophetic line is in view (see Acts 3:21, 24).

Now according to this passage, the essence of the prophet is that he has the very words of God: "I will raise up a *prophet from among their countrymen like you, and I will put My words in his mouth, and he shall speak to them all that I command him*" (v. 18). Hence, the familiar introduction of prophetic declarations in the Old Testament is, "Thus saith the Lord," which occurs over 400 times.

Since the prophet is one who speaks the very words of God, he possesses a great authority when he speaks for God: "And it shall come about that whoever will not listen to My words which he shall speak in My name, I Myself will require it of him" (Deut. 18:19). In light of this high and responsible calling of the prophet, there is a spiritual warning for those who would pretend to be prophets. God Himself would deal with such a "prophets." In fact, the most serious of civil consequences issues forth in such a situation: "But the prophet who shall speak presumptuously in My name which I have not commanded him to speak, or which he shall speak in the name of other gods, that prophet shall die" (Deut. 18:20).

---

[6] J. Ridderbos, *Deuteronomy* (BSC), trans. by Ed M. van der Maas (Grand Rapids: Regency Reference Library/Zondervan, 1951 [1984]), p. 206.

[7] A. D. H. Mayes, *Deuteronomy* (NCBC) (Grand Rapids: Wm. B. Eerdmans, 1979) p. 282.

It should further be understood that this prophetic authority is not dependent upon the prophet's recording in *writing* his prophetic oracles. The Scriptures list several non-writing prophets, such as Elijah, Elisha, Nathan, Gad, Abijah, Shemaiah, and others. Even in the New Testament era the binding nature of the apostolic-prophetic word is evident, whether it is written (i. e., prophetically inscripturated) or not (i.e., prophetically uttered). Paul's statement in 2 Thessalonians 2:15 is very clear in this regard: "So then, brethren, stand firm and hold to the traditions which you were taught, *whether by word of mouth or by letter from us.*" The obligation of the people was to both the letter *and* the word from the apostles.

> Numbers 12:6-8: Hear now My words: If there is a prophet among, you, I, the Lord, shall make Myself known to him in a vision. I shall speak with him in a dream.

This verse demonstrates that the prophet not only received divine, authoritative, revelatory prophecy by means of words, but also via dreams and visions. Such revelations are recorded by writing prophets in Isaiah 6; Jeremiah 1:11-12; 24:1; Ezekiel 1-3; 8-11; 37:1-10,40-48; Daniel 2:19; 7; 8; 10; 11; 12; Joel 2:28; Amos 7:1-9; 8:1-3; 9:1; Zechariah 1:8; 6:1-8; and elsewhere. It is clear that it is "I the Lord" who provides such visions and dreams. This will be especially significant when we enter the New Testament record. We must continually remember that God often spoke to His prophets through such phenomena as dreams and visions.

Joel 2:28-29

> And it will come about after this that I will pour out My Spirit on all mankind; and your sons and daughters will prophesy, your old men will dream dreams, your young men will see visions, and even on the male and female servants I will pour out My Spirit in those days.

This prophecy is quite important for the matter under consideration. Here we have revealed by a canonical, writing prophet that there is coming a time when the Spirit will be poured out in abundance. Such an outpouring of the Spirit will give birth to "dreams," "visions," and "prophecy." According to the explicit New Testament interpretation in Acts 2:16ff, this passage clearly speaks of the apostolic era, involving the Day of Pentecost and its repercussions recorded in Acts and the Epistles.

We should note that it mentions various forms of prophetic activity: dreams, visions, and prophecy. Here, then, a true Old Testament prophet speaks of the coming Pentecostal outpouring of the Spirit as that which results in the appearance of the same phenomena associated with the Old Testament prophets (see above on Num. 12:6). This naturally serves as the connection to the New Testament, which is especially evident in Acts 2, to which we will turn shortly.

An Alternative Interpretation?

Grudem views Joel's prediction differently. He argues that "Joel had predicted the outpouring of God's Spirit on all flesh, resulting in prophecy not just for a few people (such as those who had the authority to write the very words of Scripture), but for all God's people."[8] He notes in connection with this Moses' desire: "Would that all the Lord's people were prophets" (Num. 11:29). From this he concludes: "So 'prophet' would have been too broad a term to apply to a special, limited group of men such as the apostles, who had the unique authority to write God's words in Scripture. The New Covenant age was expected to be an age when *all* God's people would be able to prophesy."[9]

---

[8] Grudem, *Gift of Prophecy*, p. 32.
[9] Ibid. See also p. 40.

At first glance, Grudem's point seems to be well-taken. But looks are deceiving. Two fundamental problems plague his position at this point. The first is the probability that Joel's prophecy engages in prophetic hyperbole. It is doubtful that he has in mind an each-and-every universalism. Though Joel does speak of "all flesh" receiving the Spirit of God, would Grudem say "all flesh" had the Spirit poured out upon them at Pentecost?[10] Certainly not!

The hyperbole must be understood as excited, victorious, celebrational language. Rather than God's Spirit being reserved for the Jews only, it is for the Jew first, but also for the Greek. Furthermore, in the Pentecostal era (up to the destruction of the Temple, see our Acts 2 treatment below), such gifts were in great abundance, so that it might be stated hyperbolically that the gift of prophecy was given to all.

The second objection is equally strong, especially given Grudem's comments about "all" of God's people receiving prophecy.[11] Even taking "prophecy" to be what Grudem says it is (not an inspired, canon-quality revelation, but a lesser revelation from God), there are still complications for his view. We still must recognize that the prophecy spoken of in Joel 2 is that very gift which comes into the New Testament era in Acts 2 and elsewhere.

---

[10] In fact, Grudem disregards non-exact fulfillment of prophecy: "My own problem with this view [regarding Agabus, KLG] is that I find it hard to reconcile with the Old Testament pattern of precise fulfillment of prophecies . . ." (Grudem, *Gift of Prophecy*, p. 100). Consequently, he should be asked if he himself dreams dreams or sees visions (in terms of what Joel was speaking about), or if it should be the case that all Christians should.

[11] Grudem, *Gift of Prophecy*, p. 32. It should be noted that Joel predicts that the Spirit will be poured on all mankind. This pouring out (cause) results in (effect) their prophesying, dreaming dreams, and having visions. The accidental fact that "all" is not repeated before sons, daughters, young men, old men, etc., does not deny that that is precisely what is expected in the prophetic fulfillment, as Grudem's earlier quotations recognize.

Yet, as Grudem well knows, not *all* Christians actually have the gift of prophecy.[12] 1 Corinthians 12:29b asks rhetorically: "All are not prophets, are they?" And since Peter applies the Joel prophecy to the tongues-speaking at Pentecost, it would seem that we should also include tongues-speaking there, as well. Yet, Paul asks, "All do not speak with tongues, do they?" (1 Cor. 12:30b).

Acts 2:16-17

This was what was spoken of through the prophet Joel: "And it shall be in the last days," God says, "That I will pour forth of My Spirit upon all mankind; and your sons and your daughters shall prophesy, and your young men shall see visions, and your old men shall dream dreams.

The prophecy of Joel 2 is specifically cited by Peter here, in explanation of the Pentecost event. Thus, here we have prophecy of the Old Testament type (familiar Old Testament prophetic modes) entering into the New Testament era, and in fulfillment of a specific Old Testament prophet's word. And this is according to Peter's divinely inspired interpretation of Joel.

This establishes a fundamental continuity linking Old Testament and New Testament prophecy. On this basis Vos may properly speak of "the entire history of prophecy from beginning to end. The divine promise in Joel 2:28-32 extends it into the eschatological age,"[13] i.e. to the Pentecostal, New Covenant era. This divinely expected prophetic gift appears in numerous places in Acts, 1 Corinthians, and other New Testament books, as we will note in detail later.

Prophets and Apostles

As we have seen, the Scriptures indicate a divine establishment of a prophetic line (Deut. 18). That established line

---

[12] Grudem, *Gift of Prophecy*, pp. 198-200. He distinguishes between potentiality and actuality, but this is not helpful in understanding his statements I have cited above, which are categorical.

[13] Vos, *Biblical Theology*, pp. 216-217.

involves true prophets of God — Old Testament prophets — receiving revelation by words, dreams, and visions (Num. 12). Even one of the noted Old Testament writing prophets uses terms that describe his own prophecy and applies it to the Pentecost event (Joel 2; Acts 2). We can see that this demands a continuity between the Old and New Testament "prophet" and "prophecy."

But Grudem suggests that the parallel between the Testaments should be between the Old Testament prophets and the New Testament *apostles*, not the New Testament *prophets*. He argues that the apostles function more in the role of the Old Testament prophets. With this thought-provoking position, let us keep in mind our survey just presented and consider the following response.

Prophets and the Written Word

First, Grudem emphasizes the idea that "the most significant parallel between Old Testament prophets and New Testament apostles, however, is the ability to write words of Scripture, words which have absolute divine authority."[14] Elsewhere he comments: "The apostles, then, have authority to write words which are God's own words, equal in truth status and authority to the words of the Old Testament Scriptures."[15] But we should remember two important facts in this regard, which seem to undercut his rejection of continuity between the "prophets" of the Old and New Testament:

(1) In the Old Testament itself there were both writing and *non*-writing prophets. Non-writing prophets, such as Elijah, Elisha, Samuel, Nathan, Gad, Abijah, Azariah, and others, were, nevertheless, God-inspired prophets. Interestingly, Numbers 11:26-29 (a passage of significance for Grudem[16]) shows Moses refusing to quiet the (non-writing)

---

[14] Grudem, *Gift of Prophecy*, p. 27.
[15] Ibid. p. 285.
[16] Ibid. p. 32.

prophets Eldad and Medad. Instead, Moses notes that God's Spirit was upon them. Thus, the very fact that most of the Old Testament prophets were non-writing prophets would seem to militate against Grudem's view, especially when we consider that:

(2) In the New Testament there are writing and non-writing *apostles*, too. Using Grudem's own analysis, non-writing apostles include Matthias,[17] Barnabas,[18] probably Silas,[19] and possibly "even Andronicus and Juinas or a few unnamed others,"[20] as well as the remainder of "the twelve" (only Peter, John, and Matthew of "the twelve" wrote books of the New Testament). In addition, it cannot be forgotten that several of the New Testament canonical books were written by non-apostles, even in Grudem's view: "This leaves five books: Mark, Luke, Acts, Hebrews and Jude, which were not written by apostles."[21] Still further, several of the Old Testament books were written by non-prophets, as well.

We would suggest that it may be true the apostles paralleled only the *writing* prophets but not all the Old Testament prophets. The parallel would be in terms of the relatively greater and longer lasting influence of those two groups. We should consider that the writing prophets of the Old Testament are frequently mentioned in the New Testament, whereas the non-writing prophets are virtually bypassed (except for rare cases, such as Elijah).

Redemptive Historical Progress

Second, a difference in the redemptive-historical situation would account for certain differences between the Old

---

[17] Ibid. p. 271.
[18] Ibid. p. 276.
[19] Ibid. pp. 274, 276.
[20] Ibid. p. 276.
[21] Ibid. p. 286. Grudem comments elsewhere: "Luke himself is not an apostle, but his gospel is here accorded authority apparently equal with that of the apostolic writings," p. 329 (n130).

Testament Prophets and the New Testament prophets (which include both apostles and "prophets"), despite their overall continuity. Grudem explains why he believes the apostles were called "apostles" rather than "prophets." "In order to emphasize the newness of the New Covenant which Christ established, he may have deemed it appropriate to have a new name [i.e., "apostle"] to designate the first leaders of the New Covenant community, the church."[22] "Instead, a new term was chosen, 'apostle'. What we are trying to do here is show why that choice of a new term was an entirely appropriate one: it prevented much misunderstanding which would have come, not just from secular uses of the word, but even from current Jewish uses and even from the Old Testament itself."[23]

But this surely is not true, for then how could we explain so much Jewish terminology and practice employed in the apostolic era and in the New Testament itself for the Church ("elders," "deacons," "*ekklesia*," the synagogue pattern, the church as a temple, Christians as the "seed of Abraham" and the "circumcision," etc.)? A better explanation for the use of the "new" word "apostle" might be found in the different mission. The prophets of the Old Testament were mainly local, confined to Israel. As Young notes: "A prophet was a mediator between God and the theocratic nation...."[24] Harrison concurs when he writes that "it may well be that the writers concerned were thought of in the ancient Hebrew sense as mediators between God and the nation, or as representatives of God in their capacity as spokesmen to the people (cf. Exod. 4:16; 7:1; Deut. 18:15ff)."[25] The apostles, though, were commissioned to go

---

[22] Ibid. p. 39.
[23] Ibid. p. 35.
[24] Edward J. Young, *An Introduction to the Old Testament* (Grand Rapids: Wm. B. Eerdmans, 1964), p. 370.
[25] Roland Kenneth Harrison, *Introduction to the Old Testament* (Grand Rapids: Wm. B. Eerdmans, 1969), p. 269. See also: Geerhardus Vos, *Biblical Theology*, p. 370; Keil and Delitzsch, *Pentateuch*, 3:370.

out to *all* the world beyond Israel (Matt. 28:19; Acts 1:8; 13:47). The Old Testament prophets ministered God's Law to one nation; the New Testament apostles were to evangelize in all nations. The apostles were commissioned as such by one Who claimed all authority in heaven and on earth (Matt. 28:18).

Conclusion

We are more convinced of the continuity of the prophets from the Old Testament to the New Testament, than by Grudem's parallels between the Old Testament prophets and the New Testament apostles. Non-writing prophets appear in various places in both Testaments, right along side of canon writing ones.

Let us in the next chapter turn to a consideration of three major terms employed of the New Testament prophet's message.

2

Analysis Of New Testament Terms

As we continue our study of the revelatory nature of the New Testament gift of prophecy, we now turn to the complex terms applied. We have seen that the *expectation* should be one of continuity with the Old Testament prophets. As we survey the New Testament Greek lexicons on NT prophecy, we discover confirmation for our view that the OT and NT prophets have the same kind of gifts.

Several important terms associated with revelatory prophecy occur in conjunction with the New Testament prophetic gift. The most important ones are of three families:

(1) The prophecy word group, including: *prophetia*, "prophecy"), *propheteuo*, "prophesy"), and *prophetes*, "prophet").

(2) The revelation word group, including: *apokalupto*, "reveal") and *apokalupsis*, "revelation."

(3) The term *musterion*, "mystery").

In the following paragraphs we will cite noted Greek scholars to gain the proper lexical understanding of these significant terms.[1] Definition of terms is always essential in any theological debate. We will then consider counter arguments against our evidence.

---

[1] Not only the definitions proffered by these lexicographers should be noted, but also their biblical references in confirmation of these definitions.

The "Prophecy" Word Group

The Arndt-Gingrich *Lexicon*, the standard Greek lexicon of our era, defines the prophecy terms and confirms our position. Arndt-Gingrich notes, for instance, that *propheteuo*, means to "1. proclaim a divine revelation...Ac 2:17f (Jo 3:1); 19:6; 21:9; 1 Cor 11:4f . . .; 13:9; 14:1, 3-5, 24, 31, 39; Rv 11:3. . . ."[2] Of the word *prophetes*, we read: "prophet as the proclaimer and interpreter of the divine revelation. . . . 5. Christians, who are endowed w[ith] the gift of *propheteia* Ac 15:32; 1 Cor 14:29, 32, 37; Rv 22:6, 9. . . ."[3]

Another important lexicon is Cremer's *Biblico-Theological Lexicon of New Testament Greek*, which offers the following definitions. The word *prophetes* is commented on:

> The fact moreover that the earlier name for a prophet was *roeh*, seer, 1 Sam. 9:9, shews what really constitutes the prophet is immediate intercourse with God, a divine communication of what a prophet has to declare. This is further confirmed by the relation of the *apokaluptesthai* to the *propheteuein*, 1 Cor. 14:26-30. Cf. 1 Pet. 1:12 . . . Eph. 3:5.[4]

The idea is continued:

> Two things therefore go to make the prophet, an insight granted by God, into divine secrets or mysteries, and a communication to others of these secrets. . . . Accordingly in Eph. 3:5; 2:20, the prophets named side by side with apostles as the foundation of the N.T. church, are to be understood as exclusively N.T. prophets, named again in Eph. 4:11 between apostles and evangelists. See 1 Cor. 12:28, and *euangelistes*. N.T. prophets were for the Christian church what O.T. prophets were for Israel, in as much as they maintained intact the immediate connection between the church

---

[2] W. F. Arndt and F. W. Gingrich, *A Greek-English Lexicon of the New Testament* (Chicago: University of Chicago, 1957), p. 730.

[3] Ibid., pp. 730-731.

[4] Hermann Cremer, *Biblico-Theological Lexicon of New Testament Greek*, Trans. by D. W. Simon and William Urwick (Edinburgh: T and T Clark, 1872), p. 601.

and not the Holy Spirit in her but the God of her salvation above her. . . .[5]

Joseph Thayer, in his *Greek-English Lexicon*, concurs when he explains that the verb *propheteuo* means "to prophesy, i.e. to be a prophet, speak forth by divine inspiration; to predict . . ., c. to utter forth, declare, a thing which can only be known by divine revelation . . ., d. to break forth under sudden impulse in lofty discourse or in praise of divine counsels . . .; —or under the like prompting, to teach, refute, reprove, admonish, comfort others (see *prophetes*, II. 1f.), 1 Co. 11:4, 5; 13:9; 14:1, 3, 4, 5, 24, 31, 39."[6]

Thayer's comments on the noun *prophetes* are:

> II. In the N.T. 1. one who, moved by the Spirit of God and hence his organ or spokesman, solemnly declares to men what he has received by inspiration, esp[ecially]: future events, and in particular such as relate to the cause and kingdom of God and to human salvation. The title is applied to: a. the O.T. prophets . . ., b. John the Baptist . . ., c. That illustrious prophet whom the Jews . . . expected to arise just before the Messiah's advent . . ., d. the Messiah . . ., e. univ[ersally] a man filled with the Spirit of God, who by God's authority and command in words of weight pleads the cause of God and urges the salvation of men . . . he may be known — now by his supernatural knowledge of hidden things . . ., now by his power of working miracles; such a prophet Jesus is shown to have been by the passages cited . . ., f. The prophets that appeared in the apostolic age among the Christians: . . . 1 Cor. 14:29, 37; Eph. 2:20; 3:5; 4:11. . . .[7]

When Thayer treats the word *propheteia*, he comments:

> prophecy, i.e. discourse emanating from divine inspiration and declaring the purposes of God, whether by reproving and admonishing the wicked, or comforting the afflicted, or revealing things

---

[5] Ibid., p. 602.
[6] Joseph Henry Thayer, *Greek-English Lexicon of the New Testament* (Chicago: American Book Co., 1889), p. 553.
[7] Ibid., p. 553.

hidden; esp. by foretelling future events. Used in the N.T.— of the endowment and speech of the Christian teachers called *prophetai* (see *prophetes*, II.1f.): Ro. 12:6; 1 Co. 12:10; 13:2; 14:6, 22; plur. the gifts and utterances of these prophets, 1 Co. 13:8; 1 Th. 5:20. . . .[8]

The famed *Theological Dictionary of the New Testament* recognizes the same truth: "In the NT the noun *prophetes* is by far the most common term of the group. . . . Because of the revelation imparted to him by the Spirit, the biblical prophet has a special knowledge of the future. This is true of the NT prophets too (Ac. 11:28), but especially of those of the OT. . . ."[9] Continuing in TDNT we read:

Whereas the noun *prophetes* occurs chiefly in the Gospels and Acts and is rare in Paul, the verb *propheteuo* is much more prominent in Paul. . . . a. Most comprehensively it can mean 'to proclaim the revelation, the message of God, imparted to the prophet' (1 C[orinthians] 11:4f.; 13:9; 14:1,4f., 39)."[10]

And further: "Yet prophecy is not the same as teaching. Whereas teachers expound Scripture, cherish the tradition about Jesus and explain the fundamentals of the catechism, the prophets, not bound by Scripture or tradition, speak to the congregation on the basis of revelations. . . ."[11]

From the forgoing authorities, it would seem clear that the prophecy word group as found in Scripture signifies *a revelatory impartation of divine knowledge*. Of course, in post-biblical Church history it is true that the term took on an ecclesiastical significance. That is, it is frequently employed to speak of the lesser activity of simply proclaiming God's

---

[8] Ibid., p. 552.
[9] Gerhard Friedrich, "Prophets and Prophecies in the New Testament" in G. Friedrich, *Theological Dictionary of the New Testament* (Grand Rapids: Wm. B. Eerdmans, 1968), 6:828.
[10] Ibid., p. 829.
[11] Ibid., p. 854.

Word, as when a minister preaches from the Bible. He is said to be acting "prophetically." But we must distinguish this post-biblical use of the word from its biblical definition and function.

Semantic Range

Grudem tries to circumvent the lexical evidence by observing that there is a broad semantic range for certain theological words, particularly "prophet." He argues that in secular writers of the era the term indicated something less than revelatory impartation of truth.[12] He admits that in the New Testament the word "prophet" is frequently used of "the great writing prophets of the Old Testament,"[13] which would allow that the term may indicate revelatory knowledge. But then he warns of leaping to a conclusion on this semantic basis: "But that does not tell us what 'prophet' will mean when it is applied to people other than these Old Testament prophets,"[14] such as in the case of Agabus and the Corinthian prophets.

Such an argument might seem to undercut our reliance on the lexicography just presented. With the lexicographers just noted, we do not believe it does, however. In the first place, the biblical context (the New Testament record) in which the terms descriptive of the charismatic gift occur, should predispose us — if not demand us — to adopt the biblical idea, rather than the secular one. Now this, of course, is only a predisposition, but it does require Grudem to answer.

Second, in Joel 2/Acts 2 we have an Old Testament writing prophet himself employing the word "prophecy" to describe the result of the New Covenant effusion of the Spirit. Thus, one who is an Old Testament prophet applies

---

[12] Wayne A. Grudem, *The Gift of Prophecy In the New Tesatment and Today* (Westchester, IL: Crossway Books, 1988), p. 33.
[13] Ibid., p. 38.
[14] Ibid.

18 \ Charismatic Gift of Prophecy

a term descriptive of his own activity to the New Testament event. And a New Testament apostle (Peter) does the same, when he so applies Joel's prophecy.

Third, and this is most significant, *not one* of the New Testament illustrations Grudem offers of non-inspired "prophecy" is convincing. Note his samples: (1) He cites Titus 1:12, which uses "prophet" to refer to Epimenides, a sixth century Cretan religious figure, who obviously was not inspired of God. (2) In Luke 22:64 he notes the high priest's assistants mockingly demanding that Jesus "prophesy," which surely does not mean "speak words with absolute divine authority." (3) The woman at the well perceives that Jesus is a "prophet" (John 4:19), which only indicates he knew about her husbands by a "knowledge which had not come by ordinary means."[15] But consider our responses.

Was Epimenides in Titus 1:12 a prophet? Paul refers to Epimenides as such but only in the sense that *he was thought to be a prophet by his followers*. Epimenides was not a genuinely inspired prophet and Paul would never have claimed him as such. But in Epimenides' circles he would have been thought so and his title would have been "prophet." In fact, Plato called him "a divinely inspired man"; Plutarch deemed him "a man dear to the gods."[16] Consequently, this verse should not undermine the idea of prophet we establish.

In Luke 22:64 we have a case where even Grudem admits Jesus was being "mocked." Why is it inconceivable to believe that this kangaroo court was taunting Jesus to act as a genuine prophet of God? Was not Jesus, in fact, a prophet (Luke 13:33)? Had not others declared Him to be a prophet (Matt. 21:11; Luke 7:16; John 6:14; 7:40)? Had not

---

[15] These are found on pages 38 and 39 in Grudem, *Gift of Prophecy*.

[16] Plato deals with his (alleged) prophetic activities in his *Laws* 1:642 D, E. For an excellent discussion of Titus 1:12 and Epimenides, see: William Hendriksen, *1 and 2 Timothy and Titus* (NTC) (Grand Rapids: Baker, 1957), pp. 352ff.

even the religious leaders of Israel heard Him declared to be a prophet (Matt. 13:57; 21:46; John 9:17)? Had not the Pharisees even disputed whether or not Jesus was a prophet (Luke 7:39)? When He was taunted on the cross, His claims to have "saved" others was used against Him: He, allegedly, could not "save" Himself (Matt. 27:42). It would seem that the same basic idea of mocking His claims is involved in Luke 22:64. And, if so, this should not call for a redefinition of the term "prophesy."

Fourth, it is significant that not just one, but three strong terms are applied to the gift of prophecy in the New Testament. Our view of prophecy that we are presenting is not merely a bold suggestion based on insufficient evidence derived from a lone term. Paul freely applies three different revelatory terms to the gift of New Testament prophecy: "prophecy," "revelation," and "mystery" (see below). In addition, we will see in a later chapter that the very function of such prophets underscores our argument, as well.

The "Revelation" Word Group

When we turn to a consideration of the second word group before us, we find that it is closely related to the previous one. Again let us simply survey some basic Greek authorities to illustrate our point.

The Abbott-Smith *Manual Greek Lexicon* explains the significance of the Greek verb *apokalupto* by noting: "1. in general sense..., to reveal, uncover, disclose... 2. In LXX and NT, in special sense of divine revelation:... 1 Co 2:10; 14:30...."[17]

Of the noun *apokalupsis* Abott-Smith notes: "an uncovering, laying bare.... Metaph[phorically], a revealing, revelation: a disclosure of divine truth, or a manifestation from God:... 1 Co 1:7; 14:6, 26...."[18]

---

[17] G. Abbott-Smith, *A Manual Greek Lexicon of the New Testament*, 3rd ed., (Edinburgh: T and T Clark, 1937), p. 50.
[18] Ibid.

Arndt and Gingrich explain *apokalupto* similarly, when they define it thus: "uncover, reveal, in our lit. only fig. 1. gener[erally] reveal, disclose, bring to light. . . . 2. esp[ecially] of divine revelation of certain supernatural secrets. . . . The revealers are Christ . . . and the Holy Spirit 1 Cor 2:10; 14:30; Eph. 3:5. . . ."[19] Their treatment of the noun form, *apokalupsis*, is comparable: "revelation, disclosure . . . 2. or revelations of a particular kind, through visions, etc.,: w[ith] gen[etive] of the author . . . Gal 1:12; Rv 1:1; . . . 2 Cor 12:1. . . . the secret was made known to me by revelation Eph 3:3. Cf. 1 Cor 2:4D; 14:6,26; 2 Cor 12:7."[20]

Turning again to Cremer we read of *apokalupto*: "1 Cor 14:30: . . . a divine revelation, disclosure, communication, has been made."[21] Of *apokalupsis* he observes: "1 Cor. 14:6: . . . where *ap[okalupsis]* denotes the isolated communication of new facts; *gnosis* the knowledge of existing revelations; *propheteia* the application of existing and new revelations."[22]

Another major lexical tool is John M'Clintock and James Strong's *Cyclopaedia of Biblical, Theological, and Exegetical Literature*. In this work we read: "Revelation (*apokalupsis*), a disclosure of something that was before unknown; and divine revelation is the direct communication of truths before unknown from God to men. The disclosure may be made by dream, vision, oral communication, or otherwise (Dan. 2:19; 1 Cor 14:26; 2 Cor. 12:1; Gal. 1:12; Rev 1:1)."[23]

The Theological Dictionary of the New Testament follows suit with the preceding Greek scholars:

> It is on the basis of an *apokalupsis* after the manner of Ac. 16:9f. that [Paul] goes to Jerusalem to confer with the apostles (Gl. 2:2).

---

[19] Arndt and Gingrich, *Lexicon*, p. 91.
[20] Ibid.
[21] Cremer, *Lexicon*, p. 342.
[22] Ibid.
[23] John M'Clintock and James Strong's *Cyclopaedia of Biblical, Theological, and Exegetical Literature* (Grand Rapids: Baker, 1970 [rep. 1879]), vol. 8.

He presupposes that other members of the community have similar direct revelations, and he classifies these with *gnosis*, *propheteia*, and *didache*, and sets them in juxtaposition with glossolalia (1 C[or.] 14:6, 26, 30). He promises his readers, and desires for them, that by special revelation they will come to deeper knowledge (Phil. 3:15; Eph. 1:17).[24]

Thayer concurs in his analysis of the verb and noun forms of the term under scrutiny. Of *apokalupto* we read:

2. to make known, make manifest, disclose, what before was unknown; . . . . c. *apokaluptein ti tini* is used of God revealing to men things unknown . . . , especially those relating to salvation: — whether by deeds . . . ; — or by the Holy Spirit, 1 Co 2:10; 14:30; Eph. 3:5; Phil. 3:15. . . .[25]

Of *apokalupsis* we read that it means:

an uncovering. . . . 2. tropically, in N.T. and eccl. language . . . , a. a disclosure of truth, instruction, concerning divine things before unknown — esp[ecially] those relating to the Christian salvation — given to the soul by God himself, or by the ascended Christ, esp[ecially] through the operation of the Holy Spirit (1 Co. 2:10), and so to be distinguished from other methods of instruction. . . . a revelation, agreeably to a revelation received, 1 Co. 14:6; equiv[alent] to *apokekalummenon*, in the phrase [in] 1 Co. 14:26. . . .[26]

Drawing upon such lexical considerations, B. B. Warfield, discusses the idea of revelation in Scripture:

III. Modes of Revelation. 1. Modes of Revelation. . . . Under "internal suggestion" may be subsumed all the characteristic phenomena of what is most properly spoken of as "prophecy": visions and dreams, which according to a fundamental passage (Nu 12:6), constitute the typical forms of prophecy, and with them

---

[24] Albrecht Oepke, "apokalupto" in Gerhard Kittel, ed. and trans., *Theological Dictionary of the New Testament* (Grand Rapids: Wm. B. Eerdmans), 3:585.
[25] Thayer, *Lexicon*, p. 62.
[26] Ibid.

the whole "prophetic word," which shares its essential characteristic with visions and dreams, since it comes not by the will of man but from God. . . . And beyond this we have no Scriptural warrant to go on in contrasting one mode of revelation with another. Dreams may seem to us little fitted to serve as vehicles of Divine communications. But there is no suggestion in Scripture that revelations through dreams stand on a lower plane than any others; and we should not fail to remember that the essential characteristics of revelations through dreams are shared by all forms of revelation in which (whether we should call them visions or not) the images or ideas which fill, or pass in procession through, the consciousness are determined by some other power than the recipient's own will. . . . The fundamental fact in all revelation is that it is from God. . . .

2. Equal Supernaturalness of the Several Modes. . . . The objectivity of the mode of communication which is adopted is intense, and it is thrown up to observation with the greatest emphasis. Into the natural life of man God intrudes in a purely supernatural manner, bearing a purely supernatural communication. In these communications we are given accordingly just a series of "naked messages of God."[27]

That which gives to prophecy as a mode of revelation its place in the category of visions, strictly so called, and dreams is that it shares with them the distinguishing characteristic which determines the class. In them all alike the movements of the mind are determined by something extraneous to the subject's will, or rather, since we are speaking of supernaturally given dreams and visions, extraneous to the totality of the subject's own psychoses.[28]

The Term "Mystery"

The final term to which we will turn is translated in the New Testament as "mystery." This term is generally not as well known and understood by the average Christian. Nevertheless, it is a term of consequence. And, as we shall see, it carries an import harmonious with the "prophecy" and "revelation" word groups dealt with above.

Abbott-Smith's *Lexicon* comments on this term thus:

---

[27] B. B. Warfield, "Revelation", in James Orr, ed., *International Standard Bible Encyclopedia* (Grand Rapids: Wm. B. Eerdmans, 1956), 4:2577.
[28] Ibid., p. 2579.

In NT, of the counsels of God . . . , once hidden but now revealed in the Gospel or some fact thereof; (a) of the Christian revelation generally . . . ; (b) of particular truths, or details, of the Christian revelation: Ro 11:25; 1 Cor 15:51, Eph 5:23, 2 Th 2:7, Re 1:20, 17:5,7; pl[ural], *ta m[usteria].*, 1 Co 13:2, 14:2. . . .[29]

Arndt and Gingrich's lengthy treatment of the word is most interesting:

Our lit[erature] uses it to mean the secret thoughts, plans, and dispensations of God which are hidden fr[om] the human reason, as well as fr[om] all other comprehension below the divine level, and hence must be revealed to those for whom they are intended. . . .

Not all Christians are capable of understanding all the mysteries. The one who speaks in tongues *penumati lalei musteria* utters secret truths in the Spirit which he alone shares w[ith] God, and which his fellow-man, even a Christian, does not understand 1 Cor 14:2. Therefore the possession of all mysteries is a great joy 13:2. And the spirit-filled apostle can say of the highest stage of Christian knowledge, revealed only to the *teleioi: laloumen theou sophian en musterio* we impart the wisdom of God in the form of a mystery 2:7. . . .[30]

Thayer, concurs:

a hidden thing, secret, mystery. . . . In the Scriptures 1. a hidden or secret thing, not obvious to the understanding: 1 Co. 13:2; 14:2. . . . 2. a hidden purpose or counsel; secret will; . . . In the N.T., God's plan of providing salvation for men through Christ, which was once hidden but now is revealed . . .[31]

D. Miall Edwards, writing in the *International Standard Bible Encyclopedia*, notes:

---

[29] Abbott-Smith, *Lexicon*, p. 298.
[30] Arndt and Gingrich, *Lexicon*, p. 532.
[31] Thayer, *Lexicon*, p. 420.

> In the NT the word occurs 27 or ... 28 t[imes]; chiefly in Paul.... It bears its ancient sense of a revealed secret, not its modern sense of that which cannot be fathomed or comprehended.... (2) By far the most common meaning in the NT is that which is so characteristic of Paul, viz. a Divine truth once hidden, but now revealed in the gospel.... (a) It should be noted how closely "mystery" is associated with "revelation" ... as well as with words of similar import.... "Mystery" and "revelation" are in fact correlative and almost synonymous terms....[32]

In the *Zondervan Pictorial Bible Dictionary* we read: "The more common meaning of mystery in the NT, Paul's usual use of the word, is that of a divine truth once hidden, but now revealed in the Gospel.... A mystery is thus now a revelation: Christian mysteries are revealed doctrines...."[33]

The term "mystery," then, was one filled with great significance for the apostles. Its significance is directly related to the progress of redemptive history, for it speaks of God's revelation of redemptive truths for His New Covenant people. In that the prophet could speak "mysteries," he is one who was blessed with divine revelation of New Testament truth.

Conclusion

A survey of the terms employed by the apostles to speak of the gift of prophecy in the New Testament is most revealing (no pun intended!). The three terms employed, particularly by Paul, all underscore the notion of a divinely inspired utterance: "prophecy," "revelation," and "mystery." Not only do they do so individually, but the three taken together solidify our position. The clear impression left in the use of these three terms in the New Testament is that they supple-

---

[32] D. Miall Edwards, "Mystery" in James Orr, ed., *International Standard Bible Encyclopedia*, (Grand Rapids: Wm. B. Eerdmans, 1956), 3:2104, 2105.

[33] John B. Graybill, "Mystery" in M. C. Tenney, ed., *Zondervan Pictorial Bible Dictionary* (Grand Rapids: Zondervan, 1967), p. 567.

ment one another and insure a proper understanding of the gift as it appears in Scripture.

It would seem that Grudem's objections to these terms are not sufficient to overthrow their discernable lexical import. Although he sets forth some apparently strong arguments — the strongest we have seen — they are not compelling. His case would seem to be undermined further when we consider other avenues in the chapters below.

3

Authority of New Testament Prophets

The Biblical data to be presented in this chapter indicate the *extraordinary* nature of the New Testament prophet and its corollary gift, the gift of prophecy. In light of the insistence of both evangelical and Reformed theology upon the cessation of inspired revelation from God, the following data are extremely useful in demonstrating the cessation of the New Testament era prophet and gift of prophecy.

The Foundational Position of the Prophet

In Ephesians 2:19-22 the Apostle Paul provides us with insights into the foundation of the New Testament phase of the Church. Obviously, the ultimate foundation is Christ Jesus, He is called "the chief cornerstone." But in Ephesians 2:19-22 we learn that the foundation also includes the "apostles and prophets":

> So then you are no longer strangers and aliens, but you are fellow-citizens with the saints, and are of God's household, having been built upon the foundation of the apostles and prophets, Christ Jesus Himself being the corner stone, in whom the whole building, being fitted together is growing into a holy temple in the Lord; in whom you also are being built together into a dwelling of God in the Spirit.

This is a crucial passage in the debate, which deserves our careful attention.

Identifying the "Prophets"

First, the "prophets" here are indisputably the New Testament prophets, rather than the Old Testament prophets, as some have argued.[1] This may be demonstrated from a variety of angles.

1. The apostles are mentioned first, which would be unlikely if the Old Testament prophets (who preceded the apostles in history) were envisioned. In fact, in this epistle the two offices are grouped together three times, and in each of the three cases we discover this invariable order: apostles first, then prophets (2:20; 3:5; 4:11). This would seem strongly counter-suggestive to the view that the Old Testament prophets are in view here.

2. Since context is so vital to a proper interpretation of any given verse, we should note that in the very next sentence in the Greek (a mere eight verses later in the English) Paul again refers to "the apostles and the prophets." In Ephesians 3:5 his reference is unquestionably speaking of the New Testament prophets: "which in other generations was not made known to the sons of men, as it has *now* been revealed to his holy apostles and prophets in the Spirit."

The Greek word *nun* ("now") in Ephesians 3:5 speaks of a present reality, not one from antiquity. The fact that this truth was not "made known" to "other generations" to the same degree ("as"), is significant, as well. The freshness of the revelation strongly supports the contemporaneous nature of the ones to whom it was made: the prophets, as well as the apostles. Hence, they are New Testament era prophets, not Old Testament ones.

3. In Ephesians 4:11 (seven sentences later in the Greek) Paul again mentions the apostles and prophets. This time he mentions them as "gifts" granted to the Church since Christ's ascension, which is referred to in verses 8-10. In verse 7 Paul writes: "to each one of us grace was given according to the measure of Christ's *gift*." In verse 11 he continues, after a parenthetical interlude: "And He [Christ] gave some as apostles, and some as prophets, and some as

---

[1] Among older adherents to the Old Testament prophets view we could name Chrysostom, Jerome, and Calvin.

evangelists, and some as pastors and teachers." Since the prophets are gifts given, along with the apostles, as a *consequence* of Christ's victorious ascension, they must be New Testament prophets.

Unique Association with Apostles

Having noted that these prophets in Ephesians 2:20 are New Testament prophets, we now move to a *second* consideration. The "prophets" here are uniquely associated with the apostles in a very special way that neither the "evangelists" nor "pastor-teachers" of Ephesians 4:11 are associated. They evidently have a priority over these other lesser offices, for they are, *with the apostles*, a part of "the foundation" of the temple-church of God. Paul even groups both parties into one category by employing only one definite article (Gk: *to*, "the") to couple them together.

Prophets are Foundational

Third, Paul clearly speaks of these "apostles and prophets" as *foundational* to the church. All non-Pentecostal evangelicals agree that the apostles are no longer extant as an active office in the governance of the Church. A foundation, by the very nature of the case, is laid but once, while the superstructure may be erected over a long period of time.

In fact, Paul here clearly implies that the foundation is already laid. He says: "having been built upon the foundation" (*epoikodomethentes*).[2] But he goes on to speak of the building presently "growing" (*auxei*)[3] and "being built together" (*sunoikodomeisthe*)[4] on that foundation.

---

[2] *Epoikodomethentes* is in an aorist participle. God's household is already "having been built," consequently, the foundation must be there for it to have been founded upon.

[3] *Auxei* is in the present tense, which indicates ongoing activity in the present.

[4] *Sunoikodomeisthe* is in the present tense, also.

Objections

Despite the observations we have listed, there are those who disagree with the position. We shall consider some of the leading objections. Again we will employ Grudem's arguments, since they represent the most rigorous ones available.

An Alternative Interpretation

First, there is the argument from the Greek article. Grudem insists we must consider an alternative translation afforded by himself and some others. Grudem recognizes that the "prophets" here are not Old Testament prophets. He proffers a grammatical argument, however, that would suggest that this double reference speaks only of one group of people: "the grammar does not require that two groups are intended here. The same grammatical construction used here is often used in the New Testament to speak of one person or one group with two different names."[5] That is, the verse could be interpreted to say that the foundation is built upon "'his holy apostle-prophets' or 'his holy apostles who are also prophets' (one group, not two)."[6]

While it is true that this rule (the Granville-Sharp rule) does hold in a number of cases, it is not universally valid. Nor is it *required* here. Indeed, many noted New Testament scholars deny the applicability of the Granville-Sharp rule here.[7] Renowned Greek scholar, A. T. Robertson, writing in

---

[5] Wayne A. Grudem, *The Gift of Prophecy in the New Testament and Today* (Westchester, IL: Crossway Books, 1988), p. 49.

[6] Ibid., p. 51. See also p. 105.

[7] See for example: Charles Hodge, *Commentary on the Epistle to the Ephesians* (Grand Rapids: Wm. B. Eerdmans, n.d.), p. 149; Marvin R. Vincent, *The Epistles of Paul*, vol. 3 of *Word Studies in the New Testament* (Grand Rapids: Wm. B. Eerdmans, 1985 [rep. 1887]), p. 379; H. C. G. Moule, *Studies in Ephesians* (Grand Rapids: Kregal, 1977 [rep. 1893]), pp. 83-84; C. F. D. Moule, *Idiom Book of the New Testament*, 2nd. ed., (Cambridge: University Press, 1960), p. 110; William Hendriksen, *New Testament Commentary: Ephesians* (Grand Rapids: Baker, 1967), p. 141 (n74).

his massive advanced Greek grammar, uses Ephesians 2:20 as an example that: "Sometimes groups more or less distinct are treated as one for the purpose in hand, and hence use only one article."[8] Grudem himself admits "I am not implying here that it is *necessary* to translate Ephesians 2:20 and 3:5 this way, for other examples can be found where this construction does refer to two separate persons or items but it is certainly a legitimate translation, and, in the absence of contextual or other indications to the contrary, it may even be a preferable translation."[9]

Despite the grammatical *possibility* of Grudem's interpretation, the context seems to suggest otherwise. Paul mentions "apostles and prophets" three times in this short epistle. In one of those references he clearly draws a distinction between them. In Ephesians 4:11 Paul *does* use separate articles, as well as distinguishing particles (*men* and *de*): "And He gave some as apostles, and some as prophets, and some as evangelists, and some as pastors and teachers."

It would seem to require something of an anti-contextual leap of logic to suggest that at Ephesians 4:11 Paul is writing of an *altogether different* group than that of which he just had spoken by using the same exact terms in Ephesians 2:20 and 3:5. Rather, Ephesians 4:11, with its additional office-gifts, seems to be making a *progress* over his earlier references. That is, in Ephesians 2:20 and 3:5, which are found in Paul's doctrinal foundation section, Paul spoke of foundational offices of the Church. But on the basis of God's providing these revelatory foundational offices, Paul now enters into his conclusion section (beginning at Ephesians 4:1: "therefore"). At that point he begins to urge his audience to walk worthy of their calling, which calling has been inaugurated by God's gracious giving of various gifts. Those gifts include not only the two aforementioned office-

---

[8] A. T. Robertson, *A Grammar of the Greek New Testament in the Light of Historical Research* [4th ed.: Nashville: Broadman, 1934], p. 787.

[9] Grudem, *Gift of Prophecy*, p. 51.

gifts of apostles and prophets, but also ongoing office-gifts such as evangelists, pastors, and teachers.

The Reference to "Foundation" Elsewhere

Second, there is the argument from the book of Revelation. Grudem points out that there is a certain New Testament consistency in holding to an apostle-only foundation, which excludes the New Testament prophets, which prophets were found in abundance in the church at Corinth. He notes that in Revelation 21:14 John writes: "And the wall of the city had twelve foundation stones, and on them were the twelve names of the twelve apostles of the Lamb."

Though initially plausible, we believe this argument fails to provide Grudem the support he needs. He is well aware that there are more than twelve apostles, thus exceeding the number twelve employed in Revelation 21.[10] He is also aware that Christ is the chief cornerstone of the Church, though He is totally omitted in John's reference to the foundation.[11] And Grudem would surely grant that the inspired, canonical, non-apostolic writings by Luke (who in terms of word volume wrote more of the New Testament than any other writer) would be somehow foundational to the Church. Actually the symbolic requirements of the Book of Revelation (involving symmetry between the Old Testament tribes[12] and New Testament apostles) would seem to be more of an issue than John's limitation of the foundation to a certain twelve of the apostles.

More importantly, there is a fatal objection to Grudem's point. The stones in Revelation 21:14 are *not* the foundation stones to the city at all, but to the *outer wall!* Revelation 21:14 reads: "And the *wall* of the city had twelve foundation stones, and on them were the twelve names of the twelve

---

[10] Ibid., p. 272.
[11] Ibid., p. 48.
[12] It should be noted, however, that there is some difficulty with John's enumeration of the twelve tribes of Israel. In Revelation 7:4ff we have Dan omitted and Manasseh put in his place. This has generated much discussion among commentators.

apostles of the Lamb" (emphasis mine). The foundations of Ephesians 2 and Revelation 21 are two different foundations to two different structures. Grudem does not seem to notice this when he writes: "So important was this original group of twelve apostles, the 'charter members' of the office of apostle, that we read that their names are inscribed on the foundations of the heavenly city, the New Jerusalem...."[13]

The Revelation of the Mystery

Third, there is the argument from the source of the revelation of the "mystery." Of the Gentile inclusion in the New Covenant era Church (as mentioned in Eph. 3:5), Grudem remarks: "This remarkable revelation of the Gentile inclusion is many times said to come to the apostles, but is never in the New Testament said to be given to any 'prophet' or groups of prophets."[14]

In response we should note that: (1) *If* we accept Grudem's exclusion of Ephesians 3:5 as evidence for the New Testament prophets' role in revealing this truth, his argument is, in the final analysis, an argument from silence. Such arguments cannot be of the highest order of proof. Actually, precious little of what New Testament prophets spoke is recorded for us in the New Testament, and we do know they spoke *something!*

(2) The conclusion of the major New Testament debate regarding Jew and Gentile relations in the Church, which is recorded for us in Acts 15, is interesting in this regard. Luke tells us that "Judas and Silas, also being prophets themselves, encouraged and strengthened the brethren with a lengthy message" (Acts 15:32). The context, which deals with the Jerusalem Council's acceptance of the Gentiles (vv.

---

[13] Grudem, *Gift of Prophecy*, p. 271.
[14] Ibid., p. 51.

19-20), mentions that Judas and Silas had already read the letter from the Jerusalem Council (vv. 22, 30-32). What is to prevent us from supposing that they spoke by revelation of this great truth (cp. 1 Cor. 14:29-31) in supplementation to the decree itself?[15] It is obvious that the revelation of the truth through Paul and the apostles was slow in being accepted, for the problem is one of the major issues plaguing the New Covenant era Church.

(3) By Grudem's admission Luke is not an apostle.[16] That being the case, the question arises as to whether or not his writing the account in Acts 15 for the Church was a *revelation* of this mystery regarding the Gentile acceptance into the Church? Luke obviously had the gift of revelatory prophecy in that he wrote inspired, canonical Scripture. But Grudem insists that only the *apostles* were foundational to the Church and only they were involved in the revelation of the mystery to us.

A Shifting Foundation

Fourth, there is the changing foundation argument. Grudem objects that

> If the foundation consists of apostles plus all those who had the gift of prophecy in all the New Testament churches in the entire Mediterranean world, then it would have to be a 'foundation' that is continually being changed and added on to. . . . [T]his "foundation" would have more and more elements added to it as people became Christians and received spiritual gifts. . . . But all this is quite inconsistent with the metaphor of a 'foundation' which gives a picture of something that is completed before the rest of the building is begun.[17]

---

[15] It might be countered that the mystery had *already* been revealed to Paul and that these prophets, therefore, were merely repeating it. But such a rejoinder proves too much. In that case the same could be said regarding any other of the apostles, so that only Paul himself should be the foundation in this respect.

[16] Grudem, *Gift of Prophecy*, p. 329 (n130). He recognizes the problem with Luke, for he mentions it elsewhere (p. 315 [n17]).

[17] Ibid., p. 54.

Two telling objections to this point may be made. (1) Even Grudem recognizes that there were more than twelve apostles. He suggests fifteen or more.[18] And beyond the eleven original apostles (Judas, who fell from the apostolate, surely would not be counted), these extras were added *at later dates*. Paul himself was converted well after the calling of the original disciples under Jesus' ministry and after Pentecost.

We must remember that the foundation was being laid in the apostolic era. We believe the foundation was completed and not to be added to *with the close of the apostolic era*, which we also believe coincided with the completion of the writing of the canon. Holding to the integrity of divine revelation, it could not be that the new prophets (the true ones) appearing in the apostolic era Church would speak anything contradictory to the revelation through the apostles.

(2) What are we to make of Grudem's last sentence quoted above about the foundation? At Pentecost in Acts 2 we learn that "there were *added* that day about three thousand souls" (Acts 2:41) and that "the Lord was *adding to their number day by day* those who were being saved" (Acts 2:47). In Acts 4:4 we learn that they had come to be five thousand. But Paul, an apostle, was not converted until Acts 9, sometime later.

How can Grudem say: "all this is quite inconsistent with the metaphor of a 'foundation' which gives a picture of something that is completed *before the rest of the building is begun*"?[19] Are not the converts of Acts 2-8 being added to the building? If Paul is a part of the foundation (on which point we agree with Grudem), then he clearly became an apostle *after* the building was begun. Grudem inadvertently is pushing the metaphor too far.

Grudem's objections to a view such as we hold do not seem to be well grounded. Let us then continue our inves-

---

[18] Ibid., p. 272.
[19] Ibid., p. 54. Emphasis mine.

tigation into the biblical data regarding the function of the New Testament prophet.

The Significant Ranking of the Prophet

In two passages in Paul's writings where the office/gifts are listed, we find the prophets ranked just under the apostles. Ephesians 4:11 reads: "And He gave some as apostles, and some as prophets, and some as evangelists, and some as pastors and teachers." In 1 Corinthians 12:28 we read even more exactly: "And God has appointed in the church, *first* apostles, *second* prophets, third teachers, then miracles, then gifts of healings, helps, administrations, various kinds of tongues."

There seems clearly to be a design in Paul's mind in such prioritizing. He is pointing out the significance of the office-gift of prophet to the apostolic era Church. The mere mention of apostles first and prophets second in Ephesians 4:11 is suggestive of this. But the specific designation of the apostles as "first" and prophets as "second" demands a priority. And we should note that he continues the ranking beyond the second place to "third" place before slipping off into lesser priority listings introduced by "then."

In the other passage where Paul enumerates gifts, Paul begins with the gift of prophecy (see Rom. 12:6). There he does not even mention apostles, so there is no reversal of that fundamental order, but there is the preservation of that prophetic priority over other gifts. Besides, other references to prophets in Acts suggest their importance (Acts 11:27; 13:1; 15:32; 21:10). As Grudem well notes regarding 1 Corinthians 12:31: "Paul's readers would most naturally assume that the 'greater (Greek *meizon*, gifts' are those which Paul has just finished ranking 'first, second, third'. Paul's thought is then made explicit in 1 Corinthians 14:5b (RSV), where in a probably intentional use of the same word, he says that 'he who prophesies is greater'...."[20]

---

[20] Ibid., p. 69.

The Predictive Capacity of the Prophet

In Acts 2 we saw the New Testament prophet came about as a fulfillment of the prophecy of Joel 2. When we begin considering the function of the prophet in Acts (which prophets should be the same type as those in 1 Corinthians), we note that the prophet can prophesy future events. Such an activity is by definition revelational, for only God knows the future. And only God can "uncover" or "reveal" the future to man (Job 12:22; Isa. 46:8-10; Dan. 2:22). In fact, according to Deuteronomy 18:22, a key means by which to determine whether or not an alleged prophet is indeed a prophet of God is to see if what he predicts comes to pass. If it does, then God has authoritatively spoken through him.

Now what examples do we find in Acts of the prophetic capacity of the New Testament prophet? In Acts 11:27-28 we read:

> Now at this time some prophets came down from Jerusalem to Antioch. And one of them named Agabus stood up and began to indicate by the Spirit that there would certainly be a great famine all over the world. And this took place in the reign of Claudius.

In Acts 21:10-11 we read:

> And as we were staying there for some days, a certain prophet named Agabus came down from Judea. And coming to us, he took Paul's belt and bound his own feet and hands, and said, This is what the Holy Spirit says: "In this way the Jews at Jerusalem will bind the man who owns this belt and deliver him into the hands of the Gentiles."

Here, then, from a New Testament prophet we discover two instances of the ability to prophesy future events. This is compelling evidence of the revelational quality and integrity of the New Testament prophetic gift.

Objections

Before moving on to other matters, we should note that some writers attempt to circumvent the force of this argument from the predictive capacity of the prophet. Various stratagems are used against these pieces of prophecy. Let us consider the more significant ones.

Acts 11:28

Grudem points out in regard to Acts 11:28 that "a degree of imprecision is also suggested by the word translated 'foretold' (Greek *semaino*, 'signified, indicated'). . . . [W]e may conclude that absolute divine authority is neither required nor ruled out by this description."[21] The imprecision of the prophecy is suggestive more of a general Spirit induced "strong subjective sense"[22] regarding a coming occurrence than an infallible prophetic declaration along the lines of Old Testament prophecy.

But this really seems to be no countervailing argument of any consequence. First, what biblical rule states that divine prophecy has to be precise? The whole notion of an orthodox biblical theology is that of developing clarity of revelation. What is more, does not God himself suggest differing levels of clarity among those who were Old Testament prophets? In Numbers 12:6-8a we read:

> He said, "Hear now My words: If there is a prophet among you, I, the Lord, shall make Myself known to him in a vision. I shall speak with him in a dream. No so, with My servant Moses, He is faithful in all My household; With him I speak mouth to mouth, Even openly, and not in dark sayings."

Second, what are we to do with the fact that the book of Revelation was "signified" (Greek *semaino*), to John? Interestingly, in both Acts 11:28 and Rev. 1:1 the exact same tense and form of the verb is used. We are persuaded that Grudem, who believes in biblical inerrancy,[23] would not say of Revelation 1:1 "a degree of imprecision is also suggested by the word translated 'foretold' (Greek *semaino*, 'signified,

---

[21] Ibid., p. 90.
[22] Ibid., p. 92.
[23] Ibid., p. 318.

indicated')."[24] If he would not say it of Revelation 1:1, why does he seem compelled to say it of Acts 11:28?

Third, the Bible clearly states that Agabus' prophecy did come to pass: "And this took place in the reign of Claudius" (Acts 11:28b)! As Grudem puts it: "the prediction of Agabus, that there would be a famine over all the world, was fulfilled in the days of Claudius."[25] This would seem to be conclusive evidence of its inspiration.

Acts 21:4

Grudem points out that in Acts 21 there are two prophecies that could not have been a divinely inspired revelation for two fundamental reasons: (1) These prophecies were not accepted as divinely *obligatory* and (2) one did not come to pass precisely as *prophesied*.[26] These could well be formidable arguments against our position. If Grudem can make them stand, then our view may be seriously challenged.

The prophecy allegedly lacking divine obligation is found in Acts 21:4, where we read: "And after looking up the disciples, we stayed there seven days; and they kept telling Paul through the Spirit not to set foot in Jerusalem." Grudem writes of this verse that "it is significant because Paul simply disobeyed their words, something he would not have done if he had thought they were speaking the very words of God."[27]

At first blush this seems to be a strong argument against the inspired quality of prophetic knowledge, at least in this context. But in light of all the positive contrary evidence to Grudem's view, this is not as strong as it may appear. Indeed, there are several possible avenues of response that may be made to Grudem.

First, it is not inconceivable that Paul may have been in sin at this point. After all, Christ was the only sinless man

---

[24] Ibid., p. 90.
[25] Ibid., p. 99.
[26] Ibid., pp. 93-100.
[27] Ibid., p. 94.

(since Adam's fall) to walk the face of the earth. And we know from Paul's own testimony in Romans 7 that he had to struggle with temptation, with the "old man." The apostles were sinners saved by grace. It is only when they spoke under inspiration of the Spirit that they were infallible. For example, the apostles Barnabas[28] and Paul had "such a sharp disagreement [over whether to take John Mark with them] that they separated from one another" (Acts 15:39). The apostle Barnabas refused to listen to the apostle Paul "insisting that they should not take him along" (Acts 15:38). One of them, at least, had to be in the wrong. And what of the apostles Peter and Barnabas separating themselves from the gentiles for fear of the Jews (Gal. 2)? Paul even called it "hypocrisy" (Gal. 2:13) and not being "straightforward about the truth of the gospel" (Gal. 2:14). Evangelical theology must defend the inerrancy of the apostolic message, but not necessarily the conduct of the apostles themselves. Consider the example of the divinely inspired King David who also sinned grievously!

E. M. Blailock handles the difficult situation here in Acts 21:4 with these words:

> At the same time great men are not beyond the possibility of error, and Scripture is habitually frank in reporting faults and failings. The question [whether or not Paul was wrong for not heeding the exhortation of Acts 21:4] therefore remains open. Certain it is that a ministry all too short, to speak in human terms, was tragically abbreviated by the events which took place in Jerusalem, and which silenced the great voice of the apostle for vital years.[29]

Second, perhaps the context could be understood as a testing of Paul conviction to die for Christ. It may be a

---

[28] Grudem holds Barnabas to be an apostle, Ibid., p. 272.
[29] E. M. Blailock, *The Acts of the Apostles* (Grand Rapids: Wm. B. Eerdmans, 1959), p. 168.

situation something akin to Abraham almost slaying his son because God commanded it. We know from the Genesis record that God commanded Abraham to slay Isaac, but that at the last second God rescinded the command, noting that He was merely testing him.[30] Would the revelation of Paul's looming martyrdom strike fear into him?

Third, then again, perhaps the message was but a warning of the approaching trials and tribulations and nothing more. Oftentimes we are somewhat disappointed that more information is not given in Acts to fill out the picture. Acts is noted for being "rapid in its movement, sure and purposeful in brief summary or leisurely report, amazingly evocative of atmosphere, economical of words...."[31] Perhaps fuller information in verse 4 would have indicated Paul was not, in fact, being ordered by the Spirit to cease and desist from his trip to Jerusalem.

Longenecker has some interesting observations on the text that are helpful in this regard:

> The preposition 'through' of Acts 21:4, however, may just as properly be understood to signify that the Spirit's message about what would befall the apostle was the *occasion* for their urging as that the Spirit himself was *the agent*. . . . It was natural that on learning something of the difficulties ahead, his friends should try to dissuade him. Yet when he could not be persuaded, and evidently after some explanation on his part, their reply was 'the will of the Lord be done' (Acts 21:14).[32]

This sounds most reasonable, all things considered.[33] These disciples told Paul, on the basis of what they had learned about his future from the Holy Spirit's revelation,

---

[30] There are obviously fundamental differences between the two episodes: (1) Abraham heard God directly; Paul indirectly (through the disciples). (2) Abraham followed the command; Paul resisted the "command."

[31] Blailock, *Acts*, p. 12.

[32] Richard Longenecker, *The Ministry and Message of Paul* (Grand Rapids: Zondervan, 1971), p. 78.

[33] See also J. A. Alexander, *The Acts of the Apostles Explained* (New York: Anson D. F. Randolph, n.d.), 2:260. Richard B. Gaffin, *Perspectives on Pentecost* (Nutley, NJ: Presbyterian and Reformed, 1979), p. 66.

Authority of NT Prophets / 41

not to set foot in Jerusalem. With this interpretation of the events, this episode co-ordinates easily with a closely related one in Acts 21:11-12. There it is abundantly clear that the Spirit's revelation had to do with the *historical fact* of danger, not the *moral obligation* to avoid it.

Acts 21:10ff

It is argued that Agabus' prophecy was not literally fulfilled in the precise terms given. Acts 21:10-11 reads:

> And as we were staying there for some days, a certain prophet named Agabus came down from Judea. And coming to us, he took Paul's belt and bound his own feet and hands, and said, "This is what the Holy Spirit says: 'In this way the Jews at Jerusalem will bind the man who owns this belt and deliver him into the hands of the Gentiles.'"

It is alleged that this demonstrates Agabus was not a prophet on the order of the Old Testament prophets. Grudem strongly asserts:

> [T]he events of the narrative itself do not coincide with the kind of accuracy which the Old Testament requires for those who speak God's words. In fact, by Old Testament standards, Agabus would have been condemned as a false prophet, because in Acts 21:27-35 neither of his predictions are [sic] fulfilled.[34]

Grudem notes two problems with the "fulfillment" of the prophecy.[35] (1) It was not "the Jews of Jerusalem" who would "bind" Paul. Acts 21:31, 33 says: "And while they were seeking to kill him, report came up to the commander of the Roman cohort that all Jerusalem was in confusion.... Then the commander came up and took hold of him, and ordered him to be bound with two chains." (2) It was not the Jews who would "deliver" Paul into the hands of the Gentiles, they tried rather to kill him (Acts 21:31). He was

---
[34] Ibid., p. 96.
[35] Ibid., pp. 96-97.

rescued from the Jews, not delivered by them (Acts 21:32-25).

First, despite this apparent difficulty, we are clearly told, in Acts 11:28 Agabus' prophecy regarding the famine *did* take place. Was Agabus merely a good guesser, so that there in Acts 11 he was accidentally correct? Or was he an off-again, on-again prophet, with only occasional success? If so, what becomes of the Deuteronomy 18:21-22 warning about prophets whose predictions fail to come to pass? Moses certainly relied on that principle as a tool for discerning false prophecies (Num. 16:25-30).

Second, if Agabus prophesied wrongly, why did Paul not rebuke him, instead of seeking to console those whose hearts were broken at the prophecy? Acts 21:13 states "Then Paul answered, 'What are you doing, weeping and breaking my heart? For I am ready not only to be bound, but even to die at Jerusalem for the name of the Lord Jesus.'" Paul did not hesitate to call down Peter, when Peter was in error as to the truth (Gal. 2:14). After all, Agabus — on Grudem's view — had mislead the people by dogmatically saying, "This is what the Holy Spirit says." Why then does Luke record the disciples' resignation as being a resignation to "the will of the Lord" (cf. Acts 21:14)?

Third, such an argument as Grudem's requires an overly simplistic and pedantic view of prophecy and fulfillment. Despite Grudem's protestations against this point, if his own argument were valid, then much of predictive prophecy from the Old Testament could be discounted (and has been discounted by liberal theologies) on this basis.

A classic illustration of this is the fulfillment of Malachi's prophecy regarding Elijah: "Behold, I am going to send you Elijah the prophet before the coming of the great and terrible day of the Lord" (Mal. 4:5 [Heb: 3:24]). Despite this rather clear prophecy of "Elijah's" return, Jesus clearly and dogmatically informs us of the non-Elijah fulfillment of the prophecy: "I say to you, that Elijah already came, and they did not recognize him. . . . Then the disciples understood that He had spoken to them about John the Baptist" (Matt. 17:11, 12).

Again were this overly literal hermeneutic employed, Peter could be faulted for a faulty historical statement in Acts 1:18. There he stated that *Judas* purchased a field with the silver he received for betraying Christ. Matthew 27:1-7 is indisputably clear: Judas was dead when the field was purchased by *others* with his silver.

Also what would we do with the several references that say the Jews crucified Christ? This is *very much* parallel to the situation presently at hand. We know as a matter of historical record that the *Romans* were the ones who actually crucified Christ. John 19:13-16 is clear that *Pilate* "delivered Him up" to be crucified, for the Jews were not allowed the right to capital punishment (John 18:29-32). Yet, when the matter is reported by the apostles and others, we hear that the *Jews* crucified Him (Acts 2:22-23; 3:13-15; 5:30; 7:52; 1 Thess. 2:14-15). Using Grudem's pedantic approach, may we justly discount the inerrancy of Acts because "the events of the narrative itself do not coincide with the kind of accuracy"[36] which we expect from an inerrant document?

Fourth, the prophecy of Agabus in Acts 21 *was* indeed fulfilled in regard to its *fundamental point*. Paul was bound *because of* the Jews' resistance to him (cf. Acts 21:27-31, 35). The Romans would not have physically bound him if the *Jews* had not instigated the uproar that led to his binding. The weeping of the disciples was not because Jews were going to bind him rather than Romans! It was because Paul was going to be bound. All of this applies equally to Grudem's argument regarding the Jews' delivering Paul to the Gentiles. He ended up in the hands of the Gentiles, per the basic point of the prophecy.

The Voice of God in the Prophet

In keeping with the Deuteronomy 18 definition of a prophet and the Old Testament experience of the prophets,

---

[36] Phrasing from Grudem, *Gift of Prophecy*, p. 96.

it should be noted that the New Testament prophet speaks an authoritative "Thus saith the Lord." Two instances of such are recorded for us. In Acts 13:1, 2 we read:

> Now there were at Antioch, in the church that was there, prophets and teachers: Barnabas, and Simeon who was called Niger, and Lucius of Cyrene, and Manaen who had been brought up with Herod the tetrarch, and Saul. And while they were ministering to the Lord and fasting, *the Holy Spirit* said, "Set apart for Me Barnabas and Saul for the work to which I have called them."

In Acts 21:10-11 even stronger terminology is employed:

> And as we were staying there for some days, a certain prophet named Agabus came down from Judea. And coming to us, he took Paul's belt and bound his own feet and hands, and said, "*This is what the Holy Spirit says*. . . ."

It would seem clear that the words cited by these prophets were given the authority of the Holy Spirit. It would seem most reasonable to equate "This is what the Holy Spirit says" with "Thus says the Lord." But there are objections to these observations.

An unusual method of rebuttal to the view here presented is used by Grudem at this juncture. He searches through Acts and discovers eight other instances employing similar terminology to Acts 13:2 ("the Spirit said," and the like).[37] He then notes that "we find that when this form of expression is used, *if no human spokesman* is named prophecy is not in view."[38] And: "Luke's failure to attribute the speech to any one of the prophets [in Acts 13:2], coupled with his pattern elsewhere of attributing non-prophetic speech to the Holy Spirit, make it somewhat doubtful that prophecy is in view here."[39] Let us consider these observations.

---

[37] Acts 8:29; 10:19; 15:28; 16:6-7; 16:9; 18:9; 20:23; 23:9.
[38] Ibid., p. 91 (emphasis his).
[39] Ibid., p. 92.

Authority of NT Prophets / 45

First, most of these cases are indisputably divinely revelatory (and we think they all are)! And this is the crucial point to be observed of his references. For instance, Acts 8:29 says: "And *the Spirit said* to Philip, 'Go up and join this chariot.'" Acts 10:19 reads: "And while Peter was pondering the vision, the Spirit said to him, 'Behold, three men are looking for you.'" In another, Paul was spoken to by the Lord in a vision (Acts 18:9). These are not simply illuminations of the sanctified heart; these are revelations from God.

Second, another of his examples is the Jerusalem Council, which was both attended and directed by apostles: "For it seemed good to the Holy Spirit and to us . . . " (Acts 15:28). He says that there is "no indication that this was a result of prophecy."[40] But given his strong commitment to the apostles' prophetic capacity and inerrancy, how can he escape the fact that the apostles Peter (Acts 15:7), Paul (v. 12), Barnabas (v. 12), James (v. 13), and Silas (v. 22) were involved in this decision?[41] This would seem to involve prophecy, despite the fact the matter was debated.

In Acts 20:23 Paul states: "the Holy Spirit testifies to me in every city that imprisonment and afflictions await me." In this, another of his cases, Grudem is hesitant in suggesting that this "may include prophecies" because it is, he feels, ultimately "ambiguous."[42] But it would seem less ambiguous than he would allow, for we learn of several specific prophetic references by individual prophets to his coming imprisonment (Acts 21:4, 9, 12, 13).[43] And these are only the recorded ones — surely there were others, of which these would be but samples. However, did they not come to pass?

---

[40] Ibid., p. 91.
[41] All of which Grudem claims as apostles, Ibid., pp. 272, 274.
[42] Ibid., p. 91.
[43] Of Acts 21:9 Grudem comments: "No indication is given of the content of their prophecies, but the fact that prophetic warnings to Paul about suffering in Jerusalem come just before (Acts 21:4) and just after (Acts 21:11) this passage makes us think that perhaps similar warnings were contained int he prophecies given by Philip's daughters." (Ibid., p. 95)

Third, later Grudem makes an argument regarding Acts 21:4 in such a way as to undercut some of his previous argumentation. Of Acts 21:4 he notes: "This verse does not mention prophecy directly, but the parallel with Acts 11:28, where human speech activity 'through the Spirit' is explicitly attributed to the prophet Agabus, suggest that these disciples were in fact prophesying." [44]

Now if he can here make a parallel between Acts 21:4 and 11:28 (where 11:28 mentions a prophet and 21:4 does not) and equate the two phenomena as prophetic utterances, why does he not allow Acts 13:2 to be a prophecy? After all, in the very preceding verse we find that "prophets" were there (v. 1), and they were ministering when the Holy Spirit spoke (v. 2).

The Revelational Insights of the Prophet

When Paul speaks of the New Testament prophet in 1 Corinthians we discover the converging of various significant revelational terms (as surveyed above in Chapter 2). Not only do we learn the prophet speaks with a "the Holy Spirit says" (the counterpart to the Old Testament "thus saith the Lord"), but we also find the prophet to be one who "knows mysteries," "prophesies," and receives "revelation." Let us note a few key verses employing these terms. The discussion of these terms above in Chapter 2 should be recalled at this juncture.

1 Corinthians 13:2

In 1 Corinthians 13:2 we read: "And if I have the gift of prophecy, and know all mysteries and all knowledge; and if I have all faith, so as to remove mountains, but do not have love, I am nothing." Here two special gifts are mentioned: prophecy and faith (see: 1 Cor. 12:4, 7, 9). The two are kept distinct in the Greek by use of the word "if" (*ean*), which separates the various elements in verses 1, 2, and 3. Paul

---

[44] Ibid., pp. 93-94.

speaks theoretically of the person really gifted with "prophecy" as one who knows "all *mysteries* and all knowledge."

As we noted earlier, the *International Standard Bible Encyclopedia* notes that "mystery" "bears its ancient sense of a revealed secret" and that it is "a Divine truth once hidden, but now revealed in the gospel." It even observes that "It should be noted how closely 'mystery' is associated with 'revelation' . . . as well as with words of similar import. . . . 'Mystery' and 'revelation' are in fact correlative and almost synonymous terms. . . ."[45]

1 Corinthians 14:6

In 1 Corinthians 14:6 we read: "But now, brethren, if I come to you speaking in tongues, what shall I profit you, unless I speak to you either by way of revelation or of knowledge or prophecy or of teaching." Calvin's statement on this passage is helpful for our understanding Paul's structural intent here:

> I bracket revelation and prophesying together, and I think that prophesying is the servant of revelation. I take the same view about knowledge and teaching. Therefore, whatever anyone has obtained by revelation he gives out in prophesying. Teaching is the way to pass on knowledge.[46]

The point is that the gift of prophecy is rooted in the dispensing of revelation by God.

1 Corinthians 14:29-32

In 1 Corinthians 14:29-32 we read: "But let two or three prophets speak, and let the others pass judgment. But if a revelation is made to another who is seated let the first keep silent. For you can all prophesy one by one, so that all may

---

[45] D. Miall Edwards, "Mystery" in James Orr, ed., *International Standard Bible Encyclopedia*, (Grand Rapids: Wm. B. Eerdmans, 1956), 3:2104, 2105.

[46] John Calvin, *The First Epistle of Paul the Apostle to the Corinthians*, trans. by John W. Fraser, in *Calvin's Commentaries*, ed. by David W. Torrance and Thomas F. Torrance (Grand Rapids: Wm. B. Eerdmans, 1960), p. 288.

learn and all may be exhorted and the spirits of the prophets are subject to prophets." The terminology here is extremely clear: it is revelational. And this revelation is bound up with the prophetic discourse of the New Testament gift.

Ephesians 3:4-5

In Ephesians 3:4-5 we read: "And by referring to this, when you read you can understand my insight into the mystery of Christ, which in other generations was not made known to the sons of men, as it has now been revealed to His holy apostles and prophets in the Spirit." Here both "mystery" and "revelation" ("revealed") are applied to the operation of the New Testament prophet. This confluence of revelational terms relative to the New Testament prophet is most remarkable.

It is difficult to see how such revelational impartation of knowledge by the New Testament prophet can be so easily discarded. Nevertheless, there is an objection brought against our position as illustrated in the above four passages. Let us consider it from its leading evangelical proponent.

Objection

Grudem recognizes the fact that some of these terms, especially "revelation," are employed of the activity of the New Testament prophets. But he discounts their import in our argument: "While the term 'prophet' does emphasize the fact of receiving revelations from God, it in itself says nothing about the question of whether absolute divine authority attaches to the reporting of those revelations to other people.... The word 'prophet' only emphasized one particular function, the function of receiving revelation from God at this particular point."[47] He agrees that that which the prophet receives is "revelation," which "is thought by Paul to be of divine, not human, origin."[48]

---

[47] Grudem, *Gift of Prophecy*, p. 315.
[48] Ibid., p. 116.

Authority of NT Prophets / 49

Nevertheless, he denies that the revelation could be imparted to others with divine authority.

But we think his position is without merit, for at least a couple of reasons. (1) He seems unaffected by the weight of the convergence of *several* revelational terms in the activity of the non-apostolic New Testament prophet. It would seem that such a confluence of various revelational terms in Scripture demonstrates the authoritative, revelational quality of the prophetic function.

(2) His view also seems to import an arbitrary distinction into the Scriptural data. While recognizing that God imparted a "revelation" to the New Testament prophet, it asserts that there is no guarantee that that prophet would have been able to report the revelation with authority. This seems little more than a arbitrary assertion forced on the data due to a theological predisposition. Earlier he qualified his emphasis on apostolic authority: "It is *primarily* the apostles who are given the ability from the Holy Spirit to recall accurately the words and deeds of Jesus and to interpret them rightly for subsequent generations."[49] Were he able to assert and prove without qualification that the apostles were unique in this regard, his argument would carry more weight. But he cannot. As we noted earlier, Luke, who wrote more than any other New Testament writer, was not an apostle, yet his words are authoritative.

Now it may be that Grudem leans upon his observations regarding the difficulty of understanding prophecy, as evidenced in John 11:50 and 1 Peter 1:11. He notes that what the prophet sees is "often difficult to understand." He then asks, "What can we conclude from this? Apparently that the prophet *may not always understand* with complete clarity just what has been revealed to him, and at times *may not even be sure* that he has received a revelation."[50]

---

[49] Ibid., p. 28.
[50] Ibid., pp. 122, 123. See also p. 230.

But this is not helpful for distinguishing the authority of the apostles from that of the prophets, for: (1) His reference to 1 Peter 1:11 shows that even the Old Testament prophets had that difficulty.[51] (2) He notes a reference in 1 Corinthians 13 in which Paul includes himself in the matter of the difficulty of prophecy: "we know in part and we prophesy in part."[52] (3) Besides, the Apostle Peter acknowledged that some of the things the Apostle Paul wrote were "hard to understand" (2 Pet. 3:15-16).

Conclusion

As we survey the New Testament data, we discover from several angles that the New Testament prophet held a place of some significance in the apostolic church. We noted that they were placed by God as a portion of the foundation of the Church (Eph. 2:20). Consequently, they were ranked second only to the apostles themselves (1 Cor. 12:28). As such prominent and gifted members of the Church, they were able to prophesy future events, as did the prophets of old (Acts 11:27-28). In that the future is only known by God, prophets must be those who can speak a "thus saith the Lord," as, in fact, New Testament prophets do (Acts 21:10-11). In addition, they had revelational insights into the "mystery" of God (1 Cor. 13:2).

Despite well thought out objections to the view presented, Grudem's contrary arguments do not accomplish the task for which they were designed. We have weighed his most significant objections and have found them wanting. New Testament prophets could speak with revelational authority, even though most of them did not write Scripture.

---

[51] Ibid., p. 122.
[52] Ibid.

4

Alleged Problem Passages

Having presented a good deal of material in defense of the revelational character of New Testament prophecy, we turn now to a consideration of several leading passages which are arrayed against our view. Although, we have considered various stray objections up to this point, we will now concentrate our focus on these major scripture texts.

1 Corinthians 13:8-13

> Love never fails; but if there are gifts of prophecy, they will be done away; if there are tongues, they will cease; if there is knowledge, it will be done away. For we know in part, and we prophesy in part; but when the perfect comes, the partial will be done away.

Often this passage is used by charismatics themselves (and even by others who are non-charismatic) to teach that neither tongues nor prophecy will cease before the Lord returns. In light of the above demonstration of the nature of "prophecy," if the charismatic interpretation were correct, then revelation continues until Christ returns.

But this passage does not teach such. There are two basic options as to the correct interpretation of this passage. Either will effectively counter the charismatic interpretation while maintaining the cessation of the gift of prophecy. We will survey these before turning to Grudem's arguments from this passage.

Contrast of Revelational Content

In setting forth either of the views to be presented, it is important not to severe the close connection between verses

9 and 10. These are counterparts that must be understood together as expressing a unified thought, as even Grudem agrees.[1] The view which I call "Contrast of Revelational Content" may be summarized as follows.

In 1 Corinthians 13:9 we read: "we know in part (*ek merous*), and we prophesy in part." Verse 10 notes that "when the perfect (*teleion*) comes, the partial will be done away." Thus, expositors of this school of thought have argued that these miraculous gifts (and including the gift of the apostolate) served to accumulate for us only partial knowledge and prophetic understanding at best.[2] Consequently, the "partial" which will be done away with when the Lord returns is the teaching/revelation itself that came in the New Testament era via these revelational gifts.

Earlier in 1 Corinthians 13:2 Paul had facetiously (it seems) said to that clamoring (1 Cor. 1:12; 11:20-21), disorderly (1 Cor. 14:26, 33, 40), over-gifted (1 Cor. 1:7) church: "And if I have the gift of prophecy, and know all mysteries and all knowledge. . . ." Thus, he was pointing out in this passage that even all this knowledge available to the most gifted prophet will vanish away in the "complete/perfect" order brought about by the return of Christ. By so phrasing the hypothetical statement, Paul also indicated he did *not* know *all* things (even though anything he did write was inspired, infallible revelation).

In other words, the passage does not speak to the issue of when *the gift* of prophecy will cease. According to this view, even the doctrines we know from biblical revelation (that we have reserved for us by inspiration and providence) will be superceded by the eternal order and its greater fullness of knowledge. Earlier Paul spoke of this heavenly knowledge when he wrote: "things which eye has

---

[1] Wayne A. Grudem, *The Gift of Prophecy In the New Testament and Today* (Westchester, IL: Crossway Books, 1988), p. 230.

[2] See: George W. Knight III, *Prophecy in the New Testament* (Dallas, TX: Presbyterian Heritage, 1988), pp. 21-22; Richard B. Gaffin, *Perspectives on Pentecost* (Nutley, NJ: Presbyterian and Reformed, 1979), pp. 109ff.

not seen and ear has not heard, and which have not entered the heart of man, all that God has prepared for those who love Him" (1 Cor. 2:9). Surely all would agree that *in heaven* even the least of the saints knows more about divine realities than even the greatest of the apostles *while they were still on the earth*.

This is not the view of the present writer. But it is a reasonable alternative understanding of the passage that fits well within the parameters of that which we have argued to this point. Though true in its basic point (i.e., the knowledge available to those in resurrected, heavenly glory is greater even than earthly apostolic knowledge), nevertheless, there is another understanding of 1 Corinthians 13 that we believe is superior to this one.

Contrast of Revelational Mode

In that this is the view of the present writer, we will set forth this view a little more fully than the former one. This view understands the 1 Corinthians 13 passage as pointing to the providential completion of the New Testament canon as that which rendered prophecy (and other revelatory gifts, e.g., tongues and special knowledge) inoperative.

As with the preceding view, we agree that 1 Corinthians 13:9 speaks of these revelatory gifts as *piecemeal*. They are, by the very nature of the case, fragmented and incomplete revelations: "We know in part (*ek merous*), and we prophesy in part (*ek merous*)." The idea expressed here is simply this: During the age between Pentecost and the completion of the canon, God gifted a variety of believers in various churches with these revelatory gifts. But during that age those gifts were sporadic in that they gave a revelation here and one there, an epistle here, a gospel there, but did not weave a total, complete New Testament revelatory picture to any one hearer or church. The various prophetic revelations offered at best partial insight into the will of God for the Church, *while in process of revelation*.

But verse 10 speaks of something which was coming, which would contrast with the piecemeal, bit-by-bit revelation of that age. That which was to supersede the partial and do away with it was something designated "perfect." "But when the *perfect* comes, the partial will be done away." It is difficult to miss the antithetic parallel between the "partial" thing and the "perfect" ("complete, mature, full") thing. Since the "partial" speaks of prophecy and other modes of revelational insight (v. 8),[3] then it would seem that the "perfect," which would supplant these, represents the perfect and final New Testament Scripture (Jms. 1:22). This is due to the fact that modes of revelation are being purposely contrasted. Thus, it makes the man of God adequately equipped to all the tasks before him (2 Tim. 3:16-17). In other words, there is coming a time when will occur the *completion* of the revelatory process of God.[4] Until this time God's revelatory process was in gear (although there was a 400 year silence between the testaments). There would be, however, no further revelation after this era: God had spoken finally in His Son (as interpreted through His apostles, Heb. 1:1, 2; John 1:18; 14:6-9). The Old Testament looked forward to the final revelation of God's will — a revelation that was initiated through types and symbols, as well as propositional truth in the Old Testament (see Hebrews).

It is difficult to discover an argument for the cessation of Revelation with the New Testament canon, if this passage is not so understood. Any argument based upon the demise of the credentials of the apostolate, which required the necessity of seeing Christ (Acts 1:21-22) as a proof that

---

[3] See Kenneth L. Gentry, Jr., *Crucial Issues Regarding Tongues* (Mauldin, SC: GoodBirth, 1982); Merrill F. Unger, *New Testament Teaching on Tongues* (Grand Rapids: Kregal, 1971), pp. 90-101; James L. Boyer, *For A World Like Ours: Studies in 1 Corinthians* (Grand Rapids: Baker, 1971), pp. 125ff.; Robert L. Reymond, *What About Continuing Revelations and Miracles in the Presbyterian Church Today?* (n.p.: Presbyterian and Reformed, 1977), pp. 30ff.; Walter J. Chantry, *Signs of the Apostles: Observations on Pentecostalism Old and New* (Edinburgh: Banner of Truth, 1973), pp. 49ff.

[4] We even believe that this idea is contained in a proper understanding of the Daniel 9:24 statement regarding the "sealing of the vision and the prophecy." Clarke, *Clarke's Commentary*, 6 vols. (Nashville: Abingdon, n.d.), 4:602. Matthew Henry, *Matthew Henry's Commentary*, 6 vols. (Old Tappen, NJ: Revell, n.d.), 4:1094.

Alleged Problem Passages / 55

revelation does not continue, is eroded in the charismatic or charismatic-sympathetic view of this passage. Did not Paul see a *vision* of Christ? Do not the charismatic-sympathetic view allow for continuing "visions" (based on Acts 2:17ff)?

The interpretation of the intended parallel between piecemeal revelations and the perfect and complete of revelation continues in the verses following 1 Corinthians 13:9, 10. In verse 11 Paul seems to be illustrating the matter by analogy from his own physical growth: "When I was a child, I used to speak as a child, think as a child, reason, as a child; when I become a man, I did away with childish things." Notice that in verse 10 the contrast is between that which is *partial* and that which is *perfect*; whereas in verse 11 the contrast is between *childhood* and *adulthood*. In verses 8 through 10 those things which demonstrated the partial state were *three* revelatory gifts (tongues, knowledge, and prophecy); whereas in verse 11 he mentions *three* means of knowledge in the child. There seems to be a purposeful parallel between the three-fold reference to the states represented by partiality and childhood: "tongues" equal "speak as a child"; "knowledge" equals "understand as a child"; "prophesy" equals "reason as a child."

The analogy presented, then, would be this: When Paul was in his childhood, he thought as a child was expected to think. But when he became a mature man, he naturally put away childish thought modes. Similarly, when the Church was in her infancy, she operated by means of bit-by-bit, piecemeal revelation. But when she grew older, she operated by means of the finalized Scripture. Thus, tongues were related to the Church in her infancy stage (cp. 1 Cor. 14:19, 20).

Verse 12 continues the illustration of the matter by employment of another analogy: "For now we see in a mirror dimly, but then face to face; now I know in part, but then I shall know fully just as I also have been fully known." Paul here seems to be teaching the Corinthians that *now* (in *their* situation *before* the completion of the New Testament canon) they were limited to sporadic, inspired insight into the authoritative will of God. They simply did not know all God was going to reveal yet. They were, as it were, looking in a dim mirror. But when they finally have before them all the New Testament Scriptures, *then* they shall be able to fully see all they need to know, they will be able to see themselves just as they are in the sight of God (cp. Rom. 7:9-11; Jms. 1:23-25; with 1 Cor. 8:3; Gal. 4:9).[5]

Such a contrast between the occasional prophet and inscripturated revelation is not unprecedented in the Bible. In Numbers 12:6-8 this is precisely the difference God points out between the prophetic utterances of Aaron and those of Moses. Furthermore, even the apostles needed reference to Scripture and to each other. This is clear in the episode recorded in Acts 10-11 and in the Jerusalem Council in Acts 15. It is also alluded to in Peter's reference to Paul's words as being difficult to understand (2 Pet. 3:15, 16) and in Paul's desire to have the "parchments" (portions of the Scripture?) while in prison (2 Tim. 4:13).

Objections

As alluded to above, a number of evangelical scholars understand the reference to the "perfect" to be a reference to when "the Lord returns." For these scholars, this would allow that tongues, prophecy, and "knowledge" continue until that time. As Grudem notes, this is due to Paul's mention of seeing "face to face" and his knowing "as we have been fully known." The seeing "face to face," he says, seems to represent seeing God personally (as in Gen. 32:30; Exo. 33:11; Deut. 5:4; 34:10; Jdgs. 6:22; Eze. 20:35). And the being "fully known" seems to be that time after the resurrection when our knowledge is not encumbered by sin. Thus, "here then we find a definite statement about the time

---

[5] This may explain the apparent difficulty of many in the apostolic era Church in distancing themselves from Judaism (see Acts 10-11; Acts 15; Galatians: Hebrews 6; 10). The early Jewish converts were somewhat proud and racist.

of the cessation of imperfect gifts like prophecy. They will 'be made useless' or 'pass away' *when Christ returns.*"[6]

We are convinced, however, that this approach, though common among commentators, is not unassailable. We should note that Grudem's argument has to read "God" into the reference: "So when Paul says, 'But then [we shall see] face to face,' he clearly means, 'Then we shall see *God* face to face.'"[7] This does not seem to be as "clear" as he makes it sound.[8] The "face to face" references he cites from the Old Testament *specifically* mention that it is God Who is seen "face to face." Those *are* clear, but Paul does not say such. In 1 Corinthians 13 "face to face" is, in fact, adverbial, and does not mention the object. The most that can be said is that God as the object of seeing must be inferred.[9]

Furthermore, just as 1 Corinthians 13:9 and 10 compose a mutually complementary unit of thought, so do both halves of verse 12. Parts a and b of verse 12 clearly form a parallelism:
Now — we see — in a mirror; — then — face to face,
Now — we know — in part;— then — I fully know.

The context of 1 Corinthians 12-14 explains *modes of revelation,* some of which are piecemeal, as we have observed. The verse before us seems also to be dealing with revelational modes. It would seem to be putting too literal a construction on the adverbial phrase "face to face" for it to be equated with Old Testament theophanies,[10] when nothing in the context suggests it. As an adverbial phrase in the first stanza of the parallelism, "face to face" is set in opposition to "darkly in a mirror." Consequently, "face to

---

[6] Grudem, *Gift of Prophecy,* pp. 231, 232.
[7] Ibid. p. 231.
[8] Later he moderates his "clearly means" to "Paul implies," Ibid., p. 238.
[9] Wilhelm Michaelis, "*horao*", in Gerhard Kittel and Gerhard Friedrich, *Theological Dictionary of the New Testament,* vol. 5, trans. by Geoffrey W. Bromiley (Grand Rapids: Wm. B. Eerdmans, 1967), p. 344.
[10] Besides, one of Grudem's examples, Eze. 20:35, probably should not be understood of a literal face-to-face meeting anyway.

face" would seem to bear the import "plainly, *as if* face to face." And it surely is paralleling the "full knowledge" of the second stanza. Having Scripture before us is a very plain knowledge of God's will, in that evangelical Christians believe in the inspiration and perspicuity of Scripture. It is the voice of God that informs us of the will of God (John 17:17; Rom. 12:1, 2).

We should remember that Jesus promised to lead His disciples into "all truth" (surely the final revelation of God's will to man, i.e. completed scripture) later after Pentecost (John 16:13).[11] This leading to "all truth" came in pieces, being supplemented in the transitional era by sporadic prophecies; it was finalized when the last Scripture book was written. Paul's last epistle gives his stamp of approval to the totality of the final scriptural revelation: "*All* scripture is inspired of God" (2 Tim. 3:16-17).[12]

It is important to note, as well, that God gave the apostolic Church "apostles and prophets" (when mentioned invariably put first and second before other gifts/offices) for the purpose of "equipping the saints" (Eph. 4:11-12) through their instructional ministry. Through the foundational (Eph. 2:20) and revelational (Eph. 3:5) ministry of the apostles and prophets (supplemented by the teaching ministry of evangelists and pastor-teachers, Eph. 4:11) the Church, as Paul puts it in both Ephesians and 1 Corinthians, was to be carried from "infancy"[13] into "maturity/perfection."[14] As Reymond perceptively argues, the "maturity" of Ephesians 4 must come in temporal history, for it cannot be

---

[11] See also: Grudem, *Gift of Prophecy*, p. 284.
[12] It may even be that 2 Timothy is the last book of the canon to have been written. As I have argued elsewhere, Revelation, generally considered the last, probably was written in about A.D. 65, earlier than 2 Timothy. See: Kenneth L. Gentry, Jr., *Before Jerusalem Fell: Dating the Book of Revelation* (Tyler, TX: Institute for Christian Economics, 1989). Contra: Grudem, *Gift of Prophecy*, p. 238.
[13] Greek: *nepion*, cp. Eph. 4:14 with 1 Cor. 13:11.
[14] Greek: *teleios*, cp. Eph. 4:13 with 1 Cor. 13:10-11.

that in heaven there will be any danger of doctrinal error (Eph. 4:13-15).[15]

In addition, Paul is explaining the purpose of Christ's gifting the Church with apostles and prophets who would lead the Church to that maturity through their ministries (Eph. 4:11-12). They were to minister to the New Testament phase of the Church from its seminal Pentecostal beginning, through the transitional period revealed in Acts, to its final equipping with the completed Word of God, i.e. to maturity.

Grudem makes reference to the Ephesians 4 passage and notes of the gifts: "Once again, the possession of various spiritual gifts for the benefit of the whole church is *characteristic* of the New Testament age."[16] This cannot mean that *all* the gifts mentioned in the New Testament continue in this present age, for the apostolate is one of those gifts (1 Cor. 12:28-30; Eph. 4:8-12). He is aware of this, but distinguishes the apostolate as a foundational gift and writes: "We have no reason to expect that any other gifts have been replaced in this way" and therefore we should expect "the continuing experience of all the gifts."[17] Let us briefly respond.

(1) At least one other gift, the "prophet," is foundational with the apostolate, as we have shown (Chapter 3). And this, of course, is the basic issue before us. (2) If one or two of the gifts are temporary, how can it be a general principle that *all* the rest must be permanent? The principle is broken in the New Testament itself. There are still a great number of gifts available, why would prophecy have to be among them? (3) Contrary to Grudem there would seem to be ample theological and biblical justification for having

---

[15] Reymond, *What About Continuing Revelations?*, p. 35 (n12).
[16] Grudem, *Gift of Prophecy*, p. 251.
[17] Ibid.

special inaugurational-celebrational gifts associated with Christ's enthronement. In fact, the gifts mentioned in Acts 2[18] are spoken of not only as blessings for the Church, but as harbingers of the approaching Day of the Lord, which seems to be the destruction of the Temple in A.D. 70 as a divine response against Israel's rejection of Christ.[19]

In light of this, we do not believe that 1 Corinthians 13 can be used to undermine our view of the cessation of the gift of prophecy. Indeed, it enhances that view.

Ephesians 1:17 and Philippians 3:15

That the God of our Lord Jesus Christ, the Father of glory, may give to you a spirit of wisdom and revelation in the knowledge of Him (Ephesians 1:17).

Let us therefore, as many as are perfect, have this attitude; and if in anything you have a different attitude, God will reveal that also to you" (Philippians 3:15).

Frequently Ephesians 1:17 and Philippians 3:15 are brought forward as evidence either that (1) the term "revelation" may mean merely illumination, or (2) the term may speak of non-binding revelation, or (3) God promises revelation for individual believers. Let us note, however, that:

First, the obvious compelling argument against the usefulness of these passages in the present debate (i.e., whether or not revelation and prophecy continue) is that both of these were written *before* revelation ceased! There is absolutely no problem with Paul speaking in this way to Christians prior to the close of the canon.

Paul might be saying that (1) God could make a revelation to the ones needing such (as a group?). Or his meaning might be that (2) God could make a revelation on these matters to the local prophets in the church (apparently there

---

[18] Grudem refers to them in this context, Ibid., p. 250.
[19] See Gentry, *Crucial Issues Regarding Tongues*; O. Palmer Robertson, "Tongues: Sign of Covenantal Curse and Blessing," *The Presbyterian Guardian*, March, 1975 and April, 1975; J. A. Alexander, *The Acts of the Apostles Explained* (New York: Anson D. F. Randolph, 1857), 1:65-66.

were prophets "in all the churches," 1 Cor. 14:31-33). This revelatory information would be imparted to the church by prophetic disclosure as well, thus affecting those who need it.

If either of these is how this passage is to be understood, then the passage was directly applicable to the particular first century audience to which it was written and not directly applicable to us in the same way. This is much the same as Paul's admonitions to the Corinthian church not to marry (1 Cor. 7:7ff) and for women to wear veils (1 Cor. 11:2ff). These were applicable for that time, and even though coming from an inspired apostle and appearing in Scripture, are not binding as general operational principles for today.

Second, this passage actually seems to be a mild rebuke to the Philippians. Why shouldn't they believe what Paul the inspired apostle writes? Why should they have to await a later revelation from some other source? Does not Grudem make much of the fact that the apostles' directives were to be followed because as inspired revelation they were morally obligatory?[20] In the next few verses he warns of those who "walk" in a different manner than he walks (vv. 17-19). This reference to God's revealing their problems to them may be a facetious statement of the order "if I know all mysteries" (1 Cor. 13:2). This understanding (which I hold) should alleviate Grudem's objections to my first mentioned point above.[21]

Then again could it be that Paul is warning these straying church members that God will "reveal" such to them in judgment on the Judgment Day, when every man's works shall be "revealed by fire" (cp. 1 Cor. 3:13; with Phil. 3:2-4, 19; 2 Thess. 1:7-10)? This would imply more than a mild rebuke; it would be a severe warning, of the order of those in Hebrews 6 and 10.

---

[20] Grudem, *Gift of Prophecy*, pp. 85-86.
[21] Ibid., pp. 316-317.

Third, in the Ephesians 1:17 passage it should further be noted that Paul does not say: "I pray that God 'may give you a revelation'" (where "revelation" would need to be in the accusative case, rather than the genitive). Rather he says: "I pray that God 'may give you a spirit.'" This is a spirit "of wisdom and revelation."

Indeed, it is arguably the case that this should be understood to signify the *Holy Spirit*. The Holy Spirit is often called by His various attributes, e.g. "the Spirit of truth" (John 14:17), "the Holy Spirit of promise" (Eph. 1:13), and so forth.[22] This seems simply to be another way of praying for their being "filled with the Spirit" (Eph. 5:18). Thus, Paul is praying that the Ephesians might be given the Spirit (Who is the One Who revealed Scripture in the first place) so that they might be "enlightened" by the Original Author (v. 18).

1 Corinthians 14:29

Another line of argumentation often brought forward to discount the binding, authoritative nature of New Testament prophetic utterances is by reference to 1 Corinthians 14:29: "And let two or three prophets speak, and *let the other pass judgment.*" It is argued that if the prophets were bearing inspired revelation, then no one could presume to stand in judgment upon God's Word.

Grudem not only follows this approach but seeks to reinforce it by arguing that the *entire congregation* is involved in the judging process, not just particularly gifted persons, such as those with "discernment" (1 Cor. 12:10) or other "prophets." Consequently, they are to choose what is helpful for their own situations and discount what is unnecessary, which selectivity indicates a lack of authority attached to the prophecies.

---

[22] This is the view of Ephesians 1:17 held by Charles Hodge, *Commentary on the Epistle to the Ephesians* (Grand Rapids: Wm. B. Eerdmans, n.d.) pp. 71-73; William Hendriksen, *Ephesians in New Testament Commentary* (Grand Rapids: Baker, 1967), pp. 96-98; H.C.G. Moule, *Studies in Ephesians* (Grand Rapids: Kregal, 1977 [1893]), pp. 57-58; and many others.

His argument in regard to this matter is three-fold:[23] (1) Other New Testament indications suggest that the entire congregation is involved (he cites 1 Cor. 12:3; 1 Thess. 5:20-21 and makes passing reference to 1 John 4:1-6; Acts 17:11). (2) If "the rest of the prophets" is meant, Paul should have used *hoi lopoi* (Greek: "the rest"), rather than *hoi alloi* (Greek: "the others"), which suggests others in the congregation at large. (3) On the view that "the others" are restricted to prophets, we have difficulty picturing what is going on in the congregation during the prophecy. Did they just sit idly by? But this counter argument based on 1 Corinthians 14:29 is in the final analysis not convincing in light of the following considerations:

First, in the *locus classicus* dealing with the God-ordained prophet (Deut. 18:18ff), the hearers are expected to pass judgment. Deuteronomy 18:21-22 says:

> And you may say in your heart, "How shall we know the word which the Lord has not spoken?" When a prophet speaks in the name of the Lord, if the thing does not come about or come true, that is the thing which the Lord has not spoken. The prophet has spoken it presumptuously; you shall not be afraid of him.

In addition, we read of Moses setting himself up to be "judged" in Numbers 16:28-30:

> And Moses said, "By this you shall know that the Lord has sent me to do all these deeds; for this is not by doing. If these men die the death of all men, or if they suffer the fate of all men, then the Lord has not sent me. But if the Lord brings about an entirely new thing and the ground opens its mouth and swallows them up with all that is theirs and they descend alive into Sheol, then you will understand that these men have spurned the Lord."

Thus, in essence the people of Israel were to "judge" Moses and the prophets; they were to "test the spirits to see whether they be of God" (1 John 4:1). And that testing was

---

[23] Grudem, *Gift of Prophecy*, pp. 72-74.

to be based on the prophecy given, as is most clearly the case in 1 Corinthians 14:29.

Grudem, however, does not see the issue of 1 Corinthians 14:29 as one in which the *prophets* themselves were judged (as in Deut. 18), but one in which the *words* of prophets are judged, that is, sifted through to discern those words that were profitable, while discounting those that were not. He is fond of quoting the RSV rendering of 1 Corinthians 14:29, which reads: "Let two or three prophets speak, and let the others *weigh what is said*" (the emphasis is Grudem's).[24] He even notes the evaluation process is "well described by Paul's expression 'weigh what is said.'"[25]

We should note that the Revised Standard Version's "weigh what is said" phrase has no corresponding Greek backdrop; it is an interpolative and expansive rendering of one Greek word *diakrino*. This is the Greek word from which we derive "discern." According to the *Theological Dictionary of the New Testament diakrino* is often used in cases meaning to "judge between persons" (cp. Acts 15:9; 1 Cor. 4:7) and to make a distinction between objects (1 Cor. 11:29). In fact, TDNT says of 1 Corinthians 14:29: "The ref[erence] is not so much as to what the prophets say as to the spirits of the prophets, [1 Cor.] 12:10."[26] The Arndt-Gingrich *Lexicon* points to its use here as indicating: "pass judgment."[27] It equates this passage to *Didache* 11:7, which very clearly and dogmatically speaks of distinguishing between prophets.[28]

---

[24] Ibid., p. 74. He cites the RSV on pp. 72-79, 155, 193, 259.
[25] Ibid., p. 73.
[26] Friedrich Buschel, "*diakrino*," in *Theological Dictionary of the New Testament*, ed. by G. Kittel, trans. by Geoffrey W. Bromiley (Grand Rapids: Wm. B. Eerdmans, 1965), 3:947.
[27] W. F. Arndt and F. W. Gingrich, *A Greek-English Lexicon of the New Testament* (Chicago: University of Chicago, 1957), p. 184.
[28] Grudem, *Gift of Prophecy*, pp. 74, 106-107.

Alleged Problem Passages / 65

Consequently, it is a passing of judgment as to whether or not one was truly gifted to be a prophet.[29]

Second, this protective mechanism is to be expected because of New Testament warnings. Christ warned in Matthew 23:11, "Many false prophets will arise, and will mislead many." Peter warned in 2 Peter 2:1, "But false prophets also arose among the people, just as there will also be false teachers among you." Paul wrote in 1 Thessalonians 5:19-21, "Do not quench the Spirit; do not despise prophetic utterances. But examine everything carefully; hold fast to that which is good."

Grudem seems to involve himself in a subtle contradiction of sense in this regard at one point. He specifically alleges that "in both 1 Thessalonians 5:19-21 and 1 Corinthians 14:29ff. there is an absence of any warning about false prophets, a lack of any criteria for judging them and an absence of any hint of strangers coming from outside and pretending to be prophets."[30] But three pages later he comments: "Though Paul did not discuss such a possibility explicitly in 1 Corinthians, it is fair to conclude from what Paul does say that he no doubt expected that false prophets would have been detected by those with the ability to distinguish between spirits (1 Cor 12:10), and they would have betrayed themselves by their blatantly aberrant doctrine (1 Cor 12:3; 1 Jn 4:2-3)."[31] If it is "fair to conclude" Paul expected the Corinthians to be able to detect false prophets, why make an issue of his not *expressly* warning about false prophets?

Regarding the 1 Thessalonians 5 passage (which Grudem believes to be an example of discerning the good and bad elements of individual prophecies) the larger con-

---

[29] See Charles Hodge, *Commentary on the First Epistle of Paul to the Corinthians* (Grand Rapids: Wm. B. Eerdmans, 1965 [1859]), p. 302; Marvin Vincent, *Word Studies in the New Testament*, 4 vols. (Grand Rapids: Wm. B. Eerdmans, 1985 [1887]), 3:272.

[30] Grudem, *Gift of Prophecy*, p. 75.

[31] Ibid., p. 78.

text is most helpful. There was a problem at Thessalonica apparently related to false teaching, which almost certainly was traceable to false prophets. Thus, Paul emphasizes that "our gospel did not come to you in word only, but also in power and in the Holy Spirit and with full conviction; just as you know what kind of men we proved to be among you" (1 Thess. 1:5). Paul and Silvanus' teaching should have been "examined" (1 Thess. 5:21) ("discerned"? [1 Cor. 14:29]) as evidence they were true prophets. Paul and Silvanus spoke the gospel to them amid "much opposition" (1 Thess. 2:2), for "our exhortation does not come from error or impurity or by way of deceit; but just as we have been approved by God to be entrusted with the gospel, so we speak" (1 Thess. 2:2-6). Consequently, the Thessalonians received "from us the word of God's message"; they "accepted it not as the word of men, but for what it really is, the Word of God" (1 Thess. 2:13). The Thessalonians were reminded of Paul's instruction that it was God's commandment (1 Thess. 4:1-2).

Paul's urging in 1 Thessalonians 5:19-20 could then be paraphrased in modern parlance: "Just because there have been some among you who were false prophets, who sought to mislead you, do not throw out the baby with the bath water: despise not prophesying per se! Examine the many prophecies you hear, for by so doing you will be able to discern who are the true and who are the false prophets, as you have with Silvanus and me." Unfortunately, the Thessalonians were buffeted by false prophecies again later. They were alarmed that the day of the Lord had already passed (2 Thess. 2:2, 3). Nevertheless, they were to believe those things from Paul's teaching and letters (2 Thess. 2:15) over against any false guidance (prophecy?) (2 Thess. 3:1-6). Paul even pointed out that he himself had written the letter, because of the great confusion there (2 Thess. 3:17).

Continuing on with Grudem's argument from 1 Corinthians 14:29, we note that elsewhere he points out what he believes is a key distinction between this statement and the other New Testament warnings about false prophets:

> The other passages give warnings of strangers coming to the church *from outside*. . . . But in 1 Corinthians 14, Paul is talking about a meeting of those who are already accepted in the fellowship of the church ("when you come together," v. 26, RSV; "earnestly desire to prophesy", v. 39, RSV).
>
> When Paul says, "Let two or three prophets speak," he certainly does not mean that at every worship service there would be two or three more prophets newly arrived at Corinth, waiting their turn to be tested and (so they hoped) approved by the congregation. Rather, the picture is one of several prophets who are known and accepted by the congregation. . . .[32]

What may be said of this train of thought? It seems to be a serious overstatement, as will be obvious from a number of considerations: (1) Not all New Testament warnings are about unknown outsiders entering the church as corrupting agents. Second Peter 2:1, which we cited above, warns that there would be false teachers *among* (Gk: *en humin*) the people themselves. Did not John speak of "anti-christs" who "went out from us" (1 John 2:18, 19). Had Paul not warned of the danger of someone cursing Jesus by a false exercise of the gifts (1 Cor. 12:3)? Even Grudem suggests that "there were several former idolaters in the church" and that some "were saying some very disturbing things, sometimes even blaspheming Christ."[33] Will Paul not soon warn that there were some *among them* (Gk: *en humin*) teaching the most damnable heresies, i.e. that Jesus had not raised from the dead (1 Cor. 15:12, 31-34)?

(2) But despite Grudem, even at Corinth there was the danger of outside intrusion. Had Paul not spoken of an unbeliever coming in among them (1 Cor. 14:23)? Were not the problems of Corinth evidence of possible engagement of non-converted men in the life and leadership of the church (1 Cor. 3:12-15; 4:18-19; 5:1, 5, 13; 10:12; 11:28-30; 15:33-34; 16:22; 2 Cor. 11:2-5, 12-15)? Was it not common

---

[32] Ibid., p. 75.
[33] Ibid., p. 203.

practice in the first century Church to accept, house, and listen to itinerating ministers (3 John 5-8; cp. Rom. 12:13; Heb. 13:2)?

(3) Grudem presents a rather static view of the Church, when he expresses doubt that there would be in *every* service new prophets. In the first place, who is to say that this occurred in every service? Our view does not suppose such, nor does Paul's writing suggest it. But they did live in an age of rapid growth for the Church, and there might well be *frequent* arrivals of new itinerating prophets (notice that prophets traveled about, Acts 21:9, 27).

Fourth, Luke speaks favorably of the Bereans who judged (in essence) the preaching of Paul in Acts 17:11, "Now these were more noble-minded than those in Thessalonica, for they received the word with great eagerness, examining the Scriptures daily, to see whether these things were so." If they could weigh the Apostle Paul's words, why could they not be allowed the same protective privilege to weigh the words of other divinely inspired prophets?

Regarding Grudem's three-fold objection to the interpretation of 1 Corinthians 14:29 that teaches that "the others" are the other "prophets," and not the congregation at large, we should note it would not seem to matter to the overall argument we are presenting whether or not the judgment was performed at large or by a special restricted group. We do, however, believe it is exegetically justified to apply the 1 Corinthians 14:29 statement to "the other prophets." Let us respond to his arguments.

His first objection against the view that a special group (prophets not currently speaking) is expected to do the judging is not convincing. Often duties expected of a special group within the church (elders, teachers, prophets, etc.) are directed generally to the body. For instance, the Matthew 18 and 1 Corinthians 5 handling of spiritual offenders speak as if they are to be excommunicated on the basis of body-wide deliberation (Matt. 18:17; 1 Cor. 5:4, 5). But this is surely to be understood as reserved for the *officers* of the church, who act *for* the body, i.e., the "two or three gathered" (Matt.

18:19). This would seem the whole point of having elders who "rule well" (1 Tim. 5:17, 20; 1 Pet. 5:1-5), who are given a special authority over the church (Heb. 13:17; 1 Thess. 5:12). Consequently, his illustrative passages may be taken to imply the special instruction should be undertaken by the *officers* of the church, who are elected by the body.

In addition, his two leading biblical examples themselves are not compelling. 1 Corinthians 12:3 does not direct a duty at all. It simply mentions a problem. But then it is followed by a statement which would at least suggest there are special gifts for handling such problems: "Now there are diversities of gifts..." (1 Cor. 12:4). The 1 Thessalonians 5 passage is preceded by an exhortation that would suggest an *official*, rather than a general, engagement of the task could be warranted: "But we request of you, brethren, that you appreciate those who diligently labor among you, and have charge over you in the Lord and give you instruction, and that you esteem them very highly in love because of their work" (1 Thess. 5:12-13). If 1 Thessalonians 5:20-21 is not suggesting to the officers their duties, then it is informing the congregation at large of duties of the church, which the officers have apostolic warrant for enforcing.

Another of his arguments, that Paul should have used *hoi lopoi* ("the rest") if he had meant "the rest of the prophets," instead of *hoi alloi* ("the others"), is disproved by the context. (It should be noted that Grudem admits that the lexical argument is only probable.) However, the context clearly seems to nail the matter shut: The immediate context (vv. 29-33) is specifically turning its attention to the prophets. What would be so erroneous in interpreting the phrase to refer to the prophets, when he is specifically speaking of the prophets?

But more importantly, the very next verse uses the same Greek term (*allo*, the singular of *alloi*) in a way that must mean "another prophet." Notice the contextual flow: "And let two or three *prophets* speak, and let the *others* [*alloi*] pass judgment. But if a *revelation* is made to *another* [*allo*] who is seated, let the first keep silent. For you can all *prophesy* one by one ... and the spirits of *prophets* are subject to *prophets*" (1 Cor. 14:29, 33). Paul only allowed two or three prophets to speak in any given service. If there were, let us say, a dozen prophets in the church, the "other" nine should listen and discern whether the three speaking were truly prophets.

Regarding the difficulty of imagining what the congregation would be doing while an alleged prophet falsely prophesied, we have to respond simply, "So what?" Surely the officers of the church, with whom the Lord gifted the church, would be expected to act in defense of the integrity of the faith, even if it is difficult to imagine exactly how such would function. We are ignorant of a great number of the details regarding how the early church operated. How else can we explain the centuries long debate over the mode of baptism, for instance?

1 Corinthians 14:36
Was it from you that the Word of God first went forth? Or has it come to you only?

Grudem points to this verse as indicating that the prophets at Corinth did not speak God's Word. "When he says, 'Or from you did the Word of God go forth?' he implies that the Word of God has *not* gone forth from them — in other words, they have not been speaking words with absolute divine authority, like Paul has.... The Word of God 'came forth' from the apostles, not from any prophets in local churches such as Corinth."[34]

We do not think this passage is properly employed in this connection. In light of the immediate and larger context this verse should be understood as a rebuke to Corinth's self-centered pride. First Corinthians 14:37 directly addresses their spiritual pride: "If any one thinks he is a prophet or spiritual...." The Corinthians received frequent rebukes from Paul throughout the letter; they lived by their

---
[34] Ibid., pp. 83-84.

Alleged Problem Passages / 71

own rules. Consequently, Paul begins with and constantly reaffirms that they are one church in a large body of other churches (1 Cor. 1:2; 4:17; 7:17; 11:16; 14:33).

It is in this context of spiritual self-centeredness that 1 Corinthians 14:36 must be comprehended. Even granting with Grudem[35] that the word "originate" or "first" is not necessary to the translation (not being found in the Greek), our point remains. Paul is rebuking them for acting as a mother church, as if the Word of God came to the world through them! In Scripture there is an important sense in which the Word of God came from Jerusalem (Isa. 2:2-3; Mic. 4:2-3; cp. Luke 24:47; Acts 1-2). The "first" idea is not necessary to the text. Consequently, it is not necessary to understand this verse to indicate that *no* Word of God at all came from Corinth.

But then what of Grudem's assertion that the prophets could not even speak a "'Word of the Lord' on such a secondary issue as the conduct of the worship service" because "they must obey Paul and others who are able to speak with greater authority"?[36] Elsewhere he states "the implication is clear: no one at Corinth (including the prophets) could make rules which would compete with Paul's words in authority. And this would imply that no prophets at Corinth could speak 'words of the Lord' as the apostles could."[37]

How does this disprove the argument that the prophets could speak authoritatively by revelation from God? Here Paul would simply be reminding the church that there is no contradiction in God's will, and since Paul was an apostle, how could any prophet even theoretically disagree with him? Such instruction might help sort out the false prophets from the true — they searched *the words of the apostles* (Paul was known to them as an apostle, 1 Cor. 9:1,2; 2 Cor. 11:2-5,

---

[35] Ibid., p. 84.
[36] Ibid., p. 85.
[37] Ibid., p. 84.

13) to see whether these things be true, as it were. It simply does not follow logically that since "no one could make rules which would compete with Paul's words in authority" that "no prophets at Corinth could speak 'words of the Lord.'" Could *any* other true, Christ-ordained apostle speak any words that would "compete" with Paul's? The precise point is that there is no competition in God's Word! Paul wrote infallibly from the Lord, as any true prophet would know (1 Cor. 14:37-38).

The situation is something akin to that of which Vos speaks when he compares Moses to the prophets (both of whom were inspired revelators of God's will): "Moses also occupies a dominant place in the religious development of the O. T. He is placed not merely at the head of the succession of prophets, but placed over them in advance. His authority extends over subsequent ages. The latter prophets do not create anything new."[38]

1 Corinthians 11:5

Grudem brings forth an interesting argument when he turns to a consideration of the women prophets in the New Testament. In paralleling 1 Corinthians 11:5 (prophesying women should be veiled) and 1 Corinthians 14:34 (women should be in subjection to men), he discovers that since women must be subordinate to men in the congregation, therefore the prophecies of women could not be authoritative.[39]

Many commentators, traceable as far back at least as John Calvin, understand that at this point in the epistle (ch. 11) Paul is not yet handling the question of the *legitimacy* of a woman's speaking in the *formal assembly* of God's people. Paul does not turn his attention to that question until chap-

---

[38] Geerhardus Vos, *Biblical Theology: Old and New Testaments* (Grand Rapids: Wm. B. Eerdmans, 1948), p. 118.

[39] Grudem, *Gift of Prophecy*, p. 86. The case of Phillip's daughters in Acts 21:9 does not merit our attention, for there is no mention of their prophesying in a church service. Contra Grudem's discussion, *Gift of Prophecy*, pp. 95-96, 215ff.

ter 14. Here he is addressing their *conduct* at church in Corinth. That is, here he is speaking of the relationship of male to female, noting that the divine order involves the submission of the woman to the man, which submission during that day entailed veils for the woman.

Thus, without even broaching the question of the legitimacy of their women speaking in public services, Paul notes right off that whatever the case may be, the Corinthian women are out of line for the *way* they are presently conducting themselves (unveiled), which is contrary to custom and decency. Later in 1 Corinthians 14:34, while explicating prophesying in detail, he will note that it is never appropriate for a woman to speak (as a prophet or tongues-speaker) in the congregation. In the 1 Corinthians 11 context he is rebuking them for their disorderliness and unruliness in general (cp. 1 Cor. 11:17-19, 21-22, 33-34), and in verse 5 for their decorum in regard to male-female relations in particular (cp. 1 Cor. 11:16).

Conclusion

We do not believe that the various passages urged against the view that New Testament prophets bore inspired revelation to the apostolic church are properly understood in this connection. The appearance is there, to be sure, but the reality is lacking. Each of the major passages presented in opposition to our view is fully susceptible to a reasonable and contrary interpretation, which is harmonious with our view.

The New Testament prophets spoke "revelation," "mysteries," and "prophecy." These, as we have shown in earlier chapters, all speak of revelatory impartations of divine knowledge. No attempted circumvention of the significance of the prophet in the New Testament is compelling.

Part II
HISTORICAL QUESTIONS

5

A Survey Of Reformed Opinion

Being confessional and anti-gnostic, Presbyterian and Reformed thought is concerned with history and precedent. And it is thus with biblical warrant.

The Scriptures are careful to instruct the Church to preserve the historical faith once for all delivered to the saints (Jude 3). Hebrews 13:9 warns: "Do not be carried away by varied and strange teachings." Paul gives instruction to two early church leaders in this vein. To Timothy he wrote: "Retain the standard of sound words which you have heard from me, in the faith and love which are in Christ Jesus" (2 Tim 1:13). Titus was urged to be careful to see that an overseer "hold fast the faithful word which is in accord with the teaching, that he may be able to exhort in sound doctrine and to refute those who contradict" (Tit 1:9).

Although the Scriptures were completed in the first century, it has been necessary for the continuing Church of our Lord Jesus Christ to interpret and apply them. The interpretation and application of Scripture is a process — not an act. It has required the involvement of many devout men working through many centuries to systematize, compile, and disseminate the fundamental truths of Scripture.

The fact that the truth of Scripture is of no "private interpretation" (2 Pet. 1:20) is a foundational principle of Reformed thought. No interpreter of Scripture works alone. All must build on the past labors of godly predecessors. It is not the lone interpreter or group of exegetes who agree with the historic, orthodox interpretations of the past and who find themselves in the mainstream of Christian thought who are suspect. Rather, those who present novel deviations from historic Christendom are the ones who deserve careful scrutiny.

For these reasons, it is important for confessionally-based, Reformed churches to consider the historical stream of thought in which they are found for determining their position on various matters. Thus, it is helpful that the question before us (i.e., the alleged continuance of the gift of prophecy) be considered against the historical backdrop of Reformed thought. Though it is true that the question before us is ultimately a biblical and theological one, the witness of trusted and true men should have its place (secondary though it may be) in helping to point to the resolution of a matter.

The various Reformed scholars listed below give evidence supportive of our position on New Testament prophets and revelation. The fundamental elements of that view are:

(1) That the New Testament prophets were bearers of divine, inspired, infallible revelation to the first century Church, and

(2) That this office and its corresponding gift (prophecy) were limited to the apostolic era and have with the close of that era been withdrawn from the Church.

Because of space limitations only a portion of the available Reformed witnesses (and later other evangelical witnesses) will be cited. The stature of those listed should carry some weight in determining the historic Reformed position on the matter — although, as already pointed out, in the final analysis the real solution to the question is "What saith the Scriptures?" (see Chapter 1).

It should be noted that in the following citations, italics represents the original italics found in the author cited, not the emphasis of the present compiler.

A Catena of Reformed Scholarship

By way of introductory overview, we will summarily list the names of the thirty-three Reformed scholars to be quoted below:

J. A. Alexander
James Bannerman
Albert Barnes
Herman Bavinck
Louis Berkhof
James M. Boice
David Brown
John Brown
Gordon H. Clark
Leonard J. Coppes
Robert L. Dabney
John Eadie
Richard B. Gaffin, Jr.
John H. Gerstner
John Gill
Frederick L. Godet

William Hendriksen
Charles Hodge
Anthony Hoekema
R. B. Kuiper
D. Martin Lloyd-Jones
John Murray
Edwin H. Palmer
Harold F. Pellegrin
Robert Reymond
Herman Ridderbos
Thomas Scott
William G. T. Shedd
Morton H. Smith
James H. Thornwell
Benjamin B. Warfield

A Survey of Reformed Statements

1. J. A. Alexander

On Acts 2:17 Alexander comments: "To prophesy has here its usual sense, to speak by inspiration, or under a special divine influence."[1] Of Acts 13:1 he writes:

> *Prophets and Teachers* . . . i.e. either inspired teachers, as a single class, or inspired and uninspired teachers, as distinct classes. Or, still more probably than either, the two words are generic and specific terms, applied to the same persons, one denoting their divine authority, the other the precise way in which it was exercised.[2]

Regarding Acts 21:11 he points out: "*Thus* (literally, *these things*) *saith the Holy Ghost*, a formula equivalent to *Thus saith*

---

[1] J. A. Alexander, *The Acts of the Apostles*, 2 vols., (NY: Anson D. F. Randolph, 1857), 1:63.
[2] Ibid., 2:2.

the Lord in ancient prophecy, and claiming for the words of Agabus direct divine authority."³

2. James Bannerman

> The prophets of the apostolic Church are plainly to be distinguished from the apostles on the one hand, and from the evangelists on the other, among the extraordinary office-bearers, and also from both pastors and teachers among the ordinary office-bearers of the Christian society. The terms *prophecy* and *prophet*, when descriptive of this office, are plainly to be understood in the primary and more enlarged meaning of the words, as referring to an authoritative proclamation of the mind of God, whether in the shape of a revelation of Divine truth generally, or a revelation more especially of future events. There seems to be distinct enough ground for saying that the office of the prophet in the early Church comprehended both the prophecy or declaration of the Divine mind as to future events, and also the prophecy or declaration of the Divine mind as to moral or spiritual truth generally, without reference to the future.
>
> *In the first place*, the order of prophets in the New Testament Church had the same distinctive power which belonged to their brethren during the ancient dispensation, — that, namely, of foreseeing and predicting the future. . . .
>
> *In the second place*, the order of prophets in the New Testament Church had the power of declaring the mind of God generally, and without reference to the future, being inspired to preach or proclaim Divine truth, as it was revealed to them, in an extraordinary manner by the Spirit. They were infallible interpreters of the Old Testament Scriptures and inspired preachers of Divine truth, declaring the Word of God for the conversion of sinners and the profit of the Church. The difference between the prophets and the ordinary pastors or teachers of the early Church was, that the one were inspired preachers of the Gospel, and the other not inspired. The prophesying or preaching of the first was the fruit of immediate extraordinary revelation at the moment; the prophesying or preaching of the second was the fruit of their own unaided study of the Old Testament Scriptures, and personal understanding of Divine truth.⁴

---

³ Ibid., 2:265.
⁴ James Bannerman, *The Church of Christ*, 2 vols., (Edinburgh: Banner of Truth, 1869 [rep. 1960]), 2:231, 233, 234.

3. Albert Barnes

Regarding 1 Corinthians 14:29, Barnes notes of the statement "let the other judge": "And if this was a duty then, it is a duty now; if it was proper even when the teachers claimed to be under Divine inspiration, it is much more the duty of the people now."[5] Regarding 1 Corinthians 14:32 we read:

> The immediate reference of the passage is to those who are called *prophets* in the New Testament; and the interpretation should be confined to them. It is not improbable, however, that the same thing was true of the prophets of the Old Testament; and that it is really true as a general declaration of *all* the prophets whom God has inspired, that they *had* control over their own minds, and could speak or be silent at pleasure. In this the spirit of true inspiration differed essentially from the views of the heathen, who regarded themselves as driven on by a wild, controlling influence, that *compelled* them to speak even when they were unconscious of what they said.[6]

4. Herman Bavinck

> All of these offices — that of apostle, prophet, and evangelist — have vanished to the extent that their incumbents have died and they from the nature of the case have not been supplanted by any others. They were necessary in the unusual time when the church had to be established on earth. . . .
>
> Just as the apostles in their work of ruling the church as a whole received the help of the extraordinary offices of prophets and evangelists, so also in the care of each local church they were supported by the service of elders and deacons.[7]

---

[5] Albert Barnes, *Commentary on the New Testament* (Grand Rapids: Kregal, n.d. [rep. 1962]), p. 781.

[6] Ibid., p. 782.

[7] Herman Bavinck, *Our Reasonable Faith* (Grand Rapids: Wm. B. Eerdmans, 1956), p. 535.

Later he notes: "That was true of the extraordinary offices of apostle, evangelist, and prophet in the first period, instituted as they were in that first period before the establishment of the church in the world."[8]

5. James M. Boice

1. *Apostles and Prophets* . . . Some who have written about the gifts have tried to show that apostles and prophets are present today . . . [But] in these lists both *apostle* and *prophet* must be taken in their most technical sense. Therefore, *apostles* refer to those witnesses who were specifically commissioned by Christ to establish the church on a proper base, and prophets *refer* to those who received God's messages (like prophets of old) and recorded it in the pages of what we call the New Testament.

Neither one of these gifts exist today. We no longer have apostles or prophets in that sense.[9]

6. Louis Berkhof

In the New Testament the word *prophetes* is used, which is composed of *pro* and *phemi*. The preposition is not temporal in this case. Consequently, the word *prophemi* does not mean "to speak beforehand", but "to speak forth." The prophet is one who speaks forth from God. From these names, taken together, we gather that a prophet is one who sees things, that is, who receives revelations, who is in the service of God, particularly as a messenger, and who speaks in His name.[10]

7. David Brown

On Romans 12:6 Brown's comments are:

prophecy — i.e., of inspired teaching; as in Acts 15:32. Any one speaking with Divine authority — whether with reference to the past, the present, or the future — was termed a prophet (Exodus

---

[8] Ibid., p. 537.
[9] James M. Boice, *God and History*, Vol. 4 of *Foundations of the Christian Faith* (Downers Grove: Inter-Varsity Press, 1981), p. 121.
[10] L. Berkhof, *Systematic Theology*, 4th ed. (Grand Rapids: Wm. B. Eerdmans, 1941), p.358.

7:1, etc.) . . . *or he that* teacheth — Teachers are expressly distinguished from prophets, and put after them, as exercising a lower function (Acts 13:1; 1 Cor. 12:28,29).[11]

8. John Brown

"Prophecy" when spoken of as a separate gift, distinguished from the "word of wisdom" and "the word of knowledge," seems to be the supernatural knowledge of future events; but "prophets" appears to denote generally inspired teachers, who rank next to the apostles. "Prophets," however, is not a term, merely equivalent to teachers, nor is ordinary preaching to be considered the same thing as prophesying; though, as we have already seen, the teachers in the primitive Church were usually prophets, and *their* preaching was prophesying.[12]

9. Gordon H. Clark

On 1 Corinthians 12:28 Clark writes:

During the apostolic age, God also gave verbal messages to some others, including women, who were therefore prophets. Apostles and prophets are no longer with us. . . .[13]

On 1 Cor. 14:29f:

Others would escape the difficulty by denying that these prophecies were divine revelations — they were merely sermons or sermonettes. This attempt to broaden the concept of prophecy to cover any exposition of the gospel fails because 14:30 explicitly calls it a revelation, and a revelation made at the time and to the speakers.[14]

---

[11] David Brown, "Romans" in Jamieson, Fausset and Brown, *Critical and Explanatory Commentary on the Bible*, vol. 2: "New Testament" (Hartford: S. S. Scranton, n.d.), p. 252.

[12] John Brown, *Analytical Exposition of the Epistle of Paul the Apostle to the Romans* (New York: Robert Culver, 1857), pp. 451-452.

[13] Gordon Clark, *1 Corinthians: A Contemporary Commentary* (Nutley, NJ: Presbyterian and Reformed, 1975), p. 200.

[14] Ibid., p. 242.

10. Leonard J. Coppes

> We have been studying the foundation of the church. We have studied the apostles, and now we are going to consider the next office that Paul speaks of in Ephesians 2:20. He teaches that the church is founded upon the foundation of the apostles and prophets, Jesus Christ Himself being the chief cornerstone. It is clear that there can no more be new apostles than there could be another Christ. Just as His work to perfect and lay the foundation of the church was perfectly once for all accomplished, so was theirs. . . . In like manner, we have seen that if there are more prophets, there must be another Christ. If there are prophets here today, then Christ must have returned to raise up another foundational explanation of and establishing . . . of the covenant. So to think there are prophets today is to call into question the completed work of Christ . . . P.84: We find that New Testament prophets functioned as did the Old Testament prophets.[15]

11. Robert L. Dabney

Regarding the call to the minister, Dabney writes:

> The church has always held that none should preach the gospel but those who are called of God. The solid proof of this is not to be sought in those places of the Scripture where a special divine call was given to Old Testament prophets and priests, or to apostles, although such passages have been often thus misapplied. . . The call of these peculiar classes was extraordinary and by special revelation, suited to those days of theophanies and inspiration. But those days have now ceased, and God governs his church exclusively by his providence, and the Holy Spirit applying the written Scriptures.
>
> What, then, is the call to the gospel ministry? Before the answer to this question is attempted, let us protest against the vague, mystical and fanatical notions of a call which prevail in many minds, fostered, we are sorry to admit by not a little unscriptural teaching from Christians. People seem to imagine that some voice is to be heard, or some impression to be felt, or some impulse to be given to the soul, they hardly know what or whence, which is to force the man into the ministry without rational or scriptural

---

[15] Leonard J. Coppes, *Who Will Lead Us?* (Phillipsburg: Pilgrim, 1977), pp. 79, 84.

deliberation.... Is there any other expression of God's will given to us except the Bible? Where else does God authorize us to look for information as to any duty? The call to the ministry, then, is to be found, like the call of every other duty, in the teachings of God's revealed Word. The Holy Spirit has ceased to give direct revelations. He speaks to no rational adult now through any other medium than his Word, applied by his gracious light to the understanding and conscience. To look for something else is superstition. While the call of prophets and apostles was by *special revelation*, that of the gospel minister may be termed a *scriptural call*.[16]

12. John Eadie

The prophets ranked next in order to the apostles, but wanted [lacked] some of their peculiar qualifications. They spoke under the influence of the Spirit; and their instructions were infallible, so the church was built on their foundation as well as that of the apostles; 2:20... The revelation enjoyed by the apostles was communicated to prophets, 3:5.[17]

13. Richard B. Gaffin, Jr.

Apparently without exception, however, the New Testament vocabulary for prophecy is not used in this sense. There, applied to the church, it refers to a gift or function having two basic characteristics: (1) it is a gift given only to some, not all, in the church; it is a gift present on the principle of differential distribution; (2) it is a revelatory gift; that is, it brings to the church the words of God in the primary and original sense. Prophecy is not, at least primarily or as one of its necessary marks, the interpretation of an already existing inspired text or oral tradition but is itself the inspired, nonderivative Word of God.[18]

14. John H. Gerstner

In Gerstner's treatment of Ephesians 4:11 we read:

---

[16] Robert L. Dabney, *Discussions: Evangelical and Theological*, 2 vols., (Edinburgh: Banner of Truth, 1967 [rep. 1891]), 2:26, 27.

[17] John Eadie, *Commentary on the First Epistle of Paul to the Ephesians*, 2nd. ed. (London: Griffin, Bohn, and Co., 1861), p. 307.

[18] Richard B. Gaffin, Jr., *Perspectives on Pentecost* (Phillipsburg, NJ: Presbyterian and Reformed, 1979).

"Prophets." This refers to a group of men and women much more important in the New Testament economy than we often suppose. Their very listing next to the apostles themselves suggests this. They seemed to have performed both of the roles of the Old Testament prophets, namely, prediction and interpretation; or, foretelling and forthtelling, as it is sometimes put. . . Their unique office, being subordinate to that of the apostle, was also not needed after the foundation of the New Testament church had been laid. . .[19]

15. John Gill

Gill comments on 1 Corinthians 14:30:

> . . . hence it may be observed, that the custom of the primitive churches was to hear the word sitting, and the prophet or preacher stood, or sat, as he thought fit; . . . and that sometimes a revelation was made, and light conveyed to these prophets in a very sudden and extraordinary manner, when it was proper that it should be at once communicated for the good of the whole society: but this is to be understood only of those prophets or preachers, not of the common people; for it must not be thought that any that rose up, and pretended to a revelation, might be indulged to deliver it, and the speaker give way to him, which might be attended with much confusion, and many bad consequences; but only such who were know to have gifts, and who at certain times had peculiar revelations made unto them.[20]

16. Frederick L. Godet

On 1 Corinthians 14:6 we read: "Revelation, which makes the prophet, is a sudden and lively perception, produced by the Spirit's operation, of some aspect of the Divine majesty, the work of salvation; this view immediately ex-

---

[19] John H. Gerstner, *The Epistle to the Ephesians* (Grand Rapids: Baker, 1958).
[20] John Gill, *Gill's Expositor*, 9 vols., (Streamwood, Ill: Primitive Baptist Library), 8:720.

pressed in its first freshness, forms prophecy (ver. 27)."[21] On Romans 12:6 he states: "The prophet is, as it were, the eye of the church to receive new revelations."[22]

17. William Hendriksen

On Ephesians 4:11: "Prophets, again in the restricted sense (for in a broader sense every believer is a prophet), are the occasional organs of inspiration, for example, Agabus (Acts 11:28; 21:10,11). Together with the apostles they are described as being 'the church's foundation.'"[23] He expresses the same viewpoint on Romans 12:6:

> One important reason for attaching such a high value to prophesying must have been that the message of the true prophet was the product not of his own intuition or even of his own study and research but of special revelation. The prophet received his message directly from the Holy Spirit. . . So also in Acts 21:11 Agabus, one of these prophets — there were others, both men and women (Acts 13:1; 21:9) — is quoted as follows, "*The Holy Spirit says*, In this way the Jews of Jerusalem will bind the owner of this belt. . .[24]

18. Matthew Henry

At 1 Corinthians 12:28 he writes: "*Secondarily, prophets,* or persons enabled by inspiration to prophesy, interpret scripture, write by inspiration, as the evangelists did."[25] On the next verse he notes:

---

[21] F. Godet, *Commentary on St. Paul's First Epistle to the Corinthians*, 2 vols., (Edinburgh: T and T Clark, n.d.), 2:271.

[22] Ibid., 2:288.

[23] William Hendriksen, *New Testament Commentary: Ephesians* (Grand Rapids: Baker, 1967), p. 196.

[24] William Hendriksen, *New Testament Commentary: Romans* (Grand Rapids: Baker, 1981), p. 410.

[25] Matthew Henry, *Commentary on the Whole Bible*, 6 vols., (Grand Rapids: Kregal, n.d), p. 571.

As to prophesying he orders, (1) That two or three only should speak at one meeting (v. 20), and this successively, not all at once; and that the other should examine and judge what he delivered, that is, discern and determine concerning it, whether it were of divine inspiration or not. There might be false prophets, mere pretenders to divine inspiration; and the true prophets were to judge of these, and discern and discover who was divinely inspired, and by such inspiration interpreted scripture, and taught the church, and who was not — what was of divine inspiration and what was not.[26]

19. *Charles Hodge*

Regarding 1 Corinthians 12:8 he notes:

Hence, apostles and prophets are often associated as possessing the same gift, although in different degrees. "Built on the foundation of the apostles and prophets," Eph. 2:20. "As now revealed unto the holy apostles and prophets by the Spirit," Eph. 3:5; see also 4:11. The characteristic difference between these classes of officers was, that the former were endowed with permanent and plenary, the latter with occasional and partial, inspiration.[27]

Of 1 Corinthians 12:10 he writes:

To another prophecy. The nature of this gift is clearly exhibited in the 14th ch. It consisted in occasional inspiration and revelations, not merely or generally relating to the future, as in the case of Agabus, Acts 11:28, but either in some new communications relating to faith or duty, or simply an immediate impulse and aid from the Holy Spirit, in presenting truth already known, so that conviction and repentance were the effects aimed at and produced; comp. 14:25. The difference, as before stated, between the apostles and prophets, was, that the former were permanently inspired, so that their teaching was at all times infallible, whereas the prophets were infallible only occasionally. The ordinary teach-

---

[26] Ibid., 6:571.
[27] Charles Hodge, *Commentary on the First Epistle to the Corinthians* (Grand Rapids: Wm. B. Eerdmans, n.d. [1966]), p. 246.

ers were uninspired, speaking from the resources of their own knowledge and experience.[28]

On 1 Corinthians 12:28 he comments:

> Secondly, every office necessarily supposes the corresponding gift. No man could be an apostle without the gift of infallibility; nor a prophet without the gift of inspiration... Thirdly, the fact that any office existed in the apostolic church is no evidence that it was intended to be permanent. In that age there was a plentitude of spiritual manifestations and endowments demanded for the organization and propagation of the church, which is no longer required. We have no longer prophets, nor workers of miracles, nor gifts of tongues.[29]

At 1 Corinthians 13:2 we read: "*Mysteries* are secrets, things undiscoverable by human reason, which divine revelation alone can make known. And the gift of prophecy was the gift of revelation by which such mysteries were communicated; see 14:30."[30]

At 1 Corinthians 14:6 he explains: "He then varies the question, 'What shall I profit you unless I speak to you as a prophet, by (or rather *with, en*) a revelation, or as a teacher, with a doctrine.' There are not four, but only two modes of address contemplated in this verse. Revelation and prophecy belong to one; and knowledge and doctrine to the other. He who received revelations was a prophet, he who had 'the word of knowledge' was a teacher."[31]

Additional information from Hodge is available even regarding the less obvious statement of Paul in Romans 12:6:

> From these and numerous similar passages, it appears that the prophets in the Christian church were men who spoke under the

---

[28] Ibid., p. 247.
[29] Ibid., pp. 262-263.
[30] Ibid., p. 267.
[31] Ibid., p. 282.

> immediate influence of the Spirit of God, and delivered some divine communication relating to doctrinal truths, to present duty, to future events, etc., as the case might be. The point of distinction between them and the apostles, considered as religious teachers, appears to have been that the inspiration of the apostles was abiding, they were the infallible and authoritative messengers of Christ; whereas the inspiration of the prophets was occasional and transient. The latter differed from the teachers (*didaskaloi*), inasmuch as these were not necessarily inspired, but taught to others what they themselves had learned from the Scriptures, or from inspired men. Agreeably to this view of the office of the prophets, we find the sacred writers speaking of the gift of prophecy as consisting in the communication of divine truth by the Spirit of God, intended for instruction, exhortation, or consolation...
>
> The gift of which Paul here speaks, is not, therefore, the faculty of predicting future events, but that of immediate occasional inspiration, leading the recipient to deliver, as the mouth of God, the particular communication which he had received, whether designed for instruction, exhortation, or comfort.[32]

Regarding the command to prophesy "according to the proportion of faith," Hodge notes that: "It was obviously necessary that Christians, in the age of immediate inspiration, should have some means of discriminating between those who were really under the influence of the Spirit of God, and those who were either enthusiasts or deceivers."[33]

20. Anthony Hoekema

> The gift of prophecy spoken of in this chapter [i.e., 1 Cor. 14], as most commentators agree, is probably to be understood as a special charismatic gift of the Spirit whereby a person was enabled to transmit messages from God and, occasionally, to predict the future (e.g., Agabus; see Acts 11:27,28; 21:10,11). In other words,

---

[32] Charles Hodge, *Commentary on the Epistle to the Romans* (Grand Rapids: Wm. B. Eerdmans, 1886 [rep. 1972], p. 389-390.
[33] Ibid., p. 391.

we may not identify this gift with what we might call today a gift for preaching or Bible teaching.[34]

In his related book, Hoekema comments on the gifts of Romans 12:6-8: "The only gift on this list which could in some sense be thought of as miraculous is prophecy. This seems to have been a gift whereby a person was given a specific revelation from God, or enabled to explain the plan of salvation; occasionally a prophet would predict future events."[35]

21. *R. B. Kuiper*

The fact that in Ephesians 4:11 the function of evangelists is wedged in between the temporary functions of apostles and prophets and the permanent functions of pastors and teachers gives rise to the question whether evangelists were intended to serve only the apostolic church or were meant for the church of succeeding ages as well. The answer is not difficult to find. The evangelists exercised extraordinary authority, closely akin to that of the apostles.[36]

22. *D. Martin Lloyd-Jones*

[A] prophet is one who receives a direct message from God. He is one to whom the truth is revealed directly by the Spirit — not as a result of reading the Scripture or anything else, but by a direct message given, which he in turn is to impart to others. . . They had no New Testament Scriptures then; neither the Gospels nor the Epistles were available to them; but there were these people who were given spiritual truth and understanding by direct revelation and were enabled to speak it. The prophet in the Old Testa-

---

[34] Anthony Hoekema, *What About Tongue-Speaking?* (Grand Rapids: Wm. B. Eerdmans, 1966), p. 89 (n63).

[35] Anthony Hoekema, *Holy Spirit Baptism* (Grand Rapids: Wm. B. Eerdmans, 1972), p. 68.

[36] R. B. Kuiper, *God-Centered Evangelism* (Grand Rapids: Baker, 1961), p. 106.

ment did exactly the same. God revealed truth to him and enabled him to speak it. This is the characteristic of a prophet.[37]

23. J. Gresham Machen

> There have, indeed, been men in our day who have claimed to be the recipients of supernatural revelation, who have claimed to be prophets, who have said as they come forward: "Thus saith the Lord; God has spoken directly to me, and my voice is the voice of God." But those who have said that in our times are false prophets one and all; the real supernatural revelation that we know is recorded in our one blessed book, the Bible.[38]

A few pages later he makes an important observation:

> Supernatural revelation, along with the miracles, ceased when the last of the Apostles died. If you want information as to why the miracles ceased, and with them supernatural revelation, I think you will find it if you will turn, for example, to the admirable book by the late B. B. Warfield, entitled *Counterfeit Miracles*. But why should we not obtain information, in addition to that recorded in the Bible, about supernatural revelation given, indeed, not later but in Bible times? Well, it is perfectly conceivable that we might do so. It is perfectly conceivable, for example, that there might turn up in Egypt bits of papyrus affording true information about words of Jesus not contained in the four Gospels. But the bits of papyrus which have actually turned up so far hardly seem to provide such information. . . On the whole, speaking broadly, we can certainly say that all the supernatural revelation that we can be certain about, although no doubt other supernatural revelation was given in Bible times, is recorded in the pages of one book, the Bible.[39]

---

[37] D. Martyn Lloyd-Jones, *God's Way of Reconciliation* (Grand Rapids: Baker, 1972).

[38] J. Gresham Machen, *The Christian Faith in the Modern World* (Grand Rapids: Wm. B. Eerdmans, 1947), p. 29.

[39] Ibid., p. 33.

24. John Murray

In his *magnum opus*, Murray explains the Romans 12:6 statement:

> Prophecy refers to the function of communicating revelations of truth from God. The prophet was an organ of revelation; he was God's spokesman. . . the important place occupied by the gift of prophecy in the apostolic church is indicated by the prophecy of Joel fulfilled at Pentecost . . . , by the fact that prophets are next in rank to apostles, and that the church is built upon "the foundation of the apostles and prophets" (Eph. 2:20).[40]

In his perceptive article on the work of the Holy Spirit, Murray provides a careful analysis of the leading of the Holy Spirit that is helpful in our discussion:

> The basic premise upon which we must proceed is that the Word of God in the Scriptures of the Old and New Testaments is the only infallible rule of practice, as it is also the only infallible rule of faith. Complementary to this basic premise is another, namely, that the Word of God is a perfect and sufficient rule of practice. The corollary of this is that we may not look for, depend upon, or demand new revelations of the Spirit. In this respect we are in a different situation from those who lived during the era of revelation and inspiration. . .
>
> [W]e may still fall into the error of thinking that while the Holy Spirit does not provide us with special revelations in the form of words or visions or dreams, yet he may and does provide us with some *direct* feeling or impression or conviction which we are to regard as the Holy Spirit's intimation to us of what his mind and will is in a particular situation. The present writer maintains that this view of the Holy Spirit's guidance amounts, in effect, to the same thing as to believe that the Holy Spirit gives special revelation. And the reason for this conclusion is that we are, in such an event, conceiving of the Holy Spirit as giving us some special and direct communication, a communication or intimation or direction that is not mediated to us through those means which God has

---

[40] John Murray, *The Epistle to the Romans*, 2 vols., in *New International Commentary* (Grand Rapids: Wm. B. Eerdmans, 1965), 2:122.

ordained for our direction and guidance. In the final analysis this construction or conception of the Holy Spirit's guidance is in the same category as that which holds to direct and special revelation, and that for the reason that it makes little difference whether the intimation is in the form of impression or feeling or conviction or in the form of a verbal communication, if we believe that the experience which we have is a direct and special intimation to us of what the will of God is.[41]

25. *Edwin H. Palmer*

But there is another equally popular and equally fallacious practice. Some seek God's guidance not only by circumstances, but also by special revelations from the Spirit. Having studied the Word of God, they sometimes sit still and "listen." They wait for God to speak to them in the quiet hour. "Speak, Lord, for thy servant is listening" is their motto. Some apparently believe that the Spirit actually whispers in their ear. Others, however, offended by such crassness, believe that the Spirit speaks to them by hunches or impulses or mental impressions.[42]

26. *Harold F. Pellegrin*

"The prophets of both the Old and New Testament possessed abnormal insight into the will of God. . . . Both prophets received direct information through inspiration or revelation from Christ (1 Cor. 12:28; 1 Cor. 14:2, 24, 32)."[43]

27. *Robert Reymond*

Regarding 1 Corinthians 14:1:

Paul exhorts Corinthian believers to seek spiritual gifts (*ta pneumatika*), especially (*mallon de*) the gift of prophecy. The

---

[41] John Murray, *The Collected Writings of John Murray*, 4 vols., (Edinburgh: Banner of Truth, 1976), 1:186-7.

[42] Edwin H. Palmer, *The Holy Spirit* (Rev. ed.: Phillipsburg, NJ: Presbyterian and Reformed, 1973), p. 113.

[43] Harold F. Pellegrin, *The Epistle of Paul the Apostle to the Ephesians* (Grand Rapids: Zondervan, 1937), pp. 436-437.

recipient of this gift of prophecy, identified as a "prophet" in 14:29, was, as such an organ of revelation... Obviously, with the cessation of revelation at the end of the apostolic age ... there are no more prophets in this sense of the word. Consequently, Paul's injunction to seek the gift of prophecy, we would all maintain, is no longer in force. Rather, it was operative only as long as the revelatory process was still in progress. No one should be encouraged, therefore, to seek the gift of prophecy today.[44]

28. *Herman Ridderbos*

Prophecy is a special form of the Spirit given to and working in the church. For this reason the speaking of the prophets can also be called revelation (1 Cor. 14:30, cf. v. 26, v. 6, cf. Eph. 3:15), and they are mentioned together with the apostles (Eph. 3:5; cf. 2:20). This character of prophecy as revelation is to be sought in speaking under the direct impulse of the Spirit (cf. 1 Cor. 14:30), but also in the content of what is spoken in this way. The prophet receives an insight into the mysteries of God (cf. 1 Cor. 13:2); he explains the meaning and progress of the divine redemptive activity... Prophets are the Spirit-impelled proclaimers of the Word of God to the church, who unfold God's plan of redemption, as well as elucidate and impress upon it the significance of the work of God in Christ in a pastoral and paraenetic sense.[45]

29. *Thomas Scott*

On 1 Corinthians 13:8-12 Scott writes:

> But even "prophecy" would fail: the Spirit of prophecy would soon be withdrawn from the church; the instruction, given by the prophets from immediate revelation, would soon be superseded by more ordinary methods...[46]

---

[44] Robert Reymond, "Study Committee on Speaking in Tongues Report" in Paul R. Gilchrist, ed., *Documents of Synod* (Lookout Mtn., Tenn.: Reformed Presbyterian Church, Evangelical Synod, 1982), p. 367.

[45] Herman Ridderbos, *Paul: An Outline of His Theology* (Grand Rapids: Wm. B. Eerdmans, 1966 [Engl. Trans. 1975]), p. 451.

[46] Thomas Scott, *The Holy Bible With Explanatory Notes*, 3 vols., (Philadelphia: Lippincott, 1868), 3:593.

30. William G. T. Shedd

> Revelation in the restricted sense, we have seen, denotes the communication of truth or facts hitherto unknown to man, and incapable of being deduced from the structure of the human intellect, or derived through the ordinary channels of human information...
>
> In the New Testament, St. Paul describes a revelation as a species of divine communications. "What shall I profit you, except I shall speak either by revelation (*en apokalupsei*), or by knowledge," 1 Cor. 14:6. "When ye come together, every one of you hath a doctrine, hath a revelation (*apokalupsin*), hath an interpretation," 1 Cor. 14:26. "I will come to visions and revelations of the Lord," 2 Cor. 12:7. "Let a man so account of us as stewards of the mysteries of God," 1 Cor. 4:1. "Behold I show you a mystery," 1 Cor. 15:51. A mystery is a truth or fact revealed without an explanation of it. The trinity is such.[47]

Elsewhere, Shedd writes regarding Romans 12:6:

> The gift of prophecy was more than the ability to expound the Old Testament, especially the prophetical books ... The New Testament idea of the prophetic office is essentially the same as that of the Old Testament. Prophets are men who, inspired by the Spirit of God, remove the veil from the future ... ; make known concealed facts of the present, either in discovering the secret will of God ... or in disclosing the hidden thoughts of man ... etc. The difference between an apostle ... and a prophet was, that the former office was more comprehensive than the latter, and its inspiration was abiding, while the latter was occasional and transient.[48]

31. Morton H. Smith

PCA theologian, Morton Smith, testified as an expert witness in an ecclesiastical trial on the issue:

---

[47] W. G. T. Shedd, *Dogmatic Theology*, (2nd. Ed. Nashville: Thomas Nelson, 1888 [rep. 1980]), 1:77-78.
[48] W. G. T. Shedd, *Romans* (Grand Rapids: Zondervan, 1879 [1967]), p. 362.

Prosecution: "Do you think that the PCA would hold that one holding that New Testament prophecy continues and is not revelational is out of accord with Scripture?"

Dr. Smith: "The definition of prophet, of course, is the essential thing here. It seems to me that in the Bible's teaching of what a prophet is, that he is essentially a man who speaks under the inspiration of God. Certainly as you go back to it with Moses and his relationship to God, and the fact that God was going to put the words into his mouth, and then as you have those designations in the New Testament, it's interesting that you have the Church being built upon the foundation Christ Jesus the Chief Cornerstone, and the apostles and the prophets. The apostles I would judge being those with the ongoing continuing inspiration, the prophets those who would speak under inspiration, or at particular times, but not necessarily having an ongoing, continuing gift as the apostles did. But that you do see in the Bible that these two seem to be revelational, and with the foundation, that therefore those offices have ceased and that revelation has ceased with them. I do not personally see how you can maintain the office of prophet continuing without also acknowledging new revelation would come through them."[49]

32. *James H. Thornwell*

In an article entitled "The Call to the Minister" our topic is touched by Thornwell: "The principle upon which our Standards themselves seem to justify their doctrine is, that when the gifts which are essential to an office are withdrawn, the office is necessarily revoked. Miraculous gifts are indispensable to Prophets and Apostles, and, they having ceased, Prophets and Apostles have ceased with them."[50]

---

[49] Morton H. Smith, *Transcript of The Presbyterian Church in America Versus The Reverend Mr. George Stulac*, Sept. 20-21, 27, 1985 (St. Louis: Missouri Presbytery), pp. 20-21.

[50] James H. Thornwell, *The Collected Writings of James Henley Thornwell*, 4 vols., (Edinburgh: Banner of Truth, 1875 [rep. 1974]), 4:17.

33. Benjamin B. Warfield

One of the valuable features of the passage, 1 Cor. 12-14, consists in the picture given in it of Christian worship in the Apostolic age (14:26ff.). . . This, it is to be observed, was the ordinary church worship at Corinth in the Apostles' day. It is analogous in form to the freedom of our modern prayer-meeting services. What chiefly distinguishes it from them is that those who took part in it might often have a miraculous gift to exercise, "a revelation, a tongue, an interpretation," as well as "a psalm or a teaching". . . The argument may be extended to those items of the fuller list, given in 1 Cor. 12, which found less occasion for exhibition in the formal meetings for worship, but belonged more to life outside the meeting-room. That enumeration includes among the extraordinary items, you will remember, gifts of healings, workings of miracles, prophecy, discernings of spirits, kinds of tongues, the interpretation of tongues — all of which, appropriate to the worshipping assembly, are repeated in 1 Cor. 14:26ff. We are justified in considering it characteristic of the Apostolic churches that such miraculous gifts should be displayed in them. . . The Apostolic Church was characteristically a miracle working church. How long did this state of things continue? It was the characterizing peculiarity of specifically the Apostolic Church, and it belonged therefore exclusively to the Apostolic age — although no doubt this designation may be taken with some latitude. These gifts were not the possession of the primitive Christian as such; nor for that matter of the Apostolic Church or the Apostolic age for themselves; they were distinctively the authentication of the Apostles. They were part of the credentials of the Apostles as the authoritative agents of God in founding the church. Their function thus confined them to distinctively the Apostolic Church, and they necessarily passed away with it. . . The theologians of the post-Reformation era, a very clear-headed body of men, taught with great distinctness that the charismata ceased with the Apostolic age. . .[51]

Conclusion

We have listed these observations by a wide-array of noted Reformed scholars as an *historical* observation. We

---

[51] Benjamin B. Warfield, *Counterfeit Miracles* (Edinburgh: Banner of Truth, 1918 [rep. 1972]), pp. 4-6.

recognize that such a catena cannot *establish* a theological or biblical argument. Nevertheless, in that God is a creator God Who has ordained the earth and history as man's temporal abode, and in that His providence works historically, it is the Reformed Christian's concern to remain in the mainstream of orthodoxy. The innovative and unusual teachings are not so quickly accepted, unless they can be shown to have clear Scriptural warrant. Consequently, we have listed the scholarly statements above as illustrative of the mainstream of Reformed thought.

The names listed represent men greatly gifted of God and mightily used of Him in the promotion of His truth. Even if the reader disagrees with their observations, he should do so with respect, for this collection of biblical scholars represent a wide-ranging consensus of God-fearing students of Scripture. And as shown from biblical and theological arguments elsewhere, there is even a more fundamental rationale for following their observations.

6

A Survey Of Evangelical Opinion

As with the survey of Reformed scholars provided in the preceding chapter, we will begin by summarily listing the scholars to be cited in this section. After which we will record their observations related to the matter before us.

Obviously, the Reformed faith is not a law unto itself. It is a major current in the mainstream of Christian orthodoxy; it is not the totality of the current. Consequently, we should not be surprised to discover a wide-ranging evangelical concurrence with the sentiments of so many Reformed scholars. It should be borne in mind by the reader that, of course, there are evangelical scholars who disagree. Our listing will include only those names that concur with our analysis of the charismatic gift of prophecy. These, too, are eminent, God-fearing scholars.

A Catena of Evangelical Scholarship

Henry Alford
Albert Barry
F. F. Bruce
K. Burger
A. R. Fausset
Francis Foulkes
H. M. Gwatkin
S. M. Jackson
George Eldon Ladd
H. A. W. Meyer

Leon Morris
H. C. G. Moule
C. von Orelli
Philip Schaff
John R. W. Scott
Milton S. Terry
M. R. Vincent
W. E. Vine
B. F. Westcott

A Survey of Evangelical Statements

1. Henry Alford

On Acts 11:27, Alford makes the following remarks:

> *Prophetai* Inspired teachers in the early Christian church, referred to in the Acts, and in the Epistles of Paul.... The foretelling of future events was not the usual form which their inspiration took, but an *exalted and super-human teaching*, ranked by St. Paul above "speaking in tongues," in being the *utterance of their own conscious intelligence informed by the Holy Spirit*. This inspiration was, however, occasionally, as here, and ch. 21:10, made the vehicle of *prophecy*, properly so called.[1]

2. Albert Barry

> For the nature and function of prophecy in the Church, see the detailed treatment of the subject by St. Paul in 1 Cor. 14. It is sufficient here to note (1) that from very early times the "prophets" are mentioned as a separate class (see Acts 11:27; 15:32); 21:10), distinguished from teachers (Acts 13:1), and that, in this Epistle especially, they are spoken of, in connection with the Apostles, as receiving the revealed mystery of the gospel (chap. 3:5), and being ... "the foundation of the Church;" (2) that their office, like the Apostolate, is clearly extraordinary, distinct from the ordinary and permanent teaching of the evangelists and pastors, and, probably, best described by the two phrases so constantly applied to the prophets of the Old Testament — "the word of the Lord came to me;" "the Spirit of the Lord was upon me."[2]

3. F. F. Bruce

> The prophets of the apostolic age were men who from time to time spoke in the churches under the direct prompting of the Spirit of God (cf. Acts 11:27ff; 13:1 ff; 21:4, 9; 1 Cor. 14:1ff). Toward the end of the apostolic age it became increasingly necessary to test

---

[1] Henry Alford, *The Greek New Testament* (London: Longmans, Green, 1894), p. 129.

[2] Albert Barry, "Ephesians," in C. J. Ellicott, *Commentary on the Whole Bible*, 8 vols., (Grand Rapids: Zondervan, n.d. [rep]), 8:39.

the claims of these people, to see whether they spoke by the inspiration of the Spirit of God or of a very different kind of spirit (1 Jn. 4:1ff; Rev. 2:20). In the churches of the first generation the apostles and prophets discharged a unique role, which in some essential features has been taken over by the canonical writings of the New Testament.[3]

4. K. Burger

In transferring the office of the Church to her members, we thus get the wide range in which the idea of the New-Testament prophecy is to be taken. It corresponds entirely with Deut. 18:18 sq.; and thus a prophet is such a one, who is called by the spirit of God, here by the spirit of Jesus Christ, to become the organ of communicating the truth in such a manner that his testimony, with convincing power of the truth, proves itself to the hearers as the Word of God. . . .[4]

5. A. R. Faussett

Regarding 1 Corinthians 12:28, Faussett comments: *"teachers — who taught, for the most part, truths already revealed; whereas, the prophets made new revelations, and spoke all their prophesyings under the Spirit's influence."*[5]

On 1 Corinthians 14:1 we read:

"but rather — "but chiefly that ye may prophesy" (speak and exhort under inspiration) . . . whether as to future events, i.e., strict prophecy, or explaining obscure parts of Scripture, especially the prophetical Scriptures, or illustrating and setting forth questions of Christian doctrine and practice. Our modern *preaching* is the successor of *prophecy*, but without the inspiration.[6]

---

[3] F. F. Bruce, *The Epistle to the Ephesians* (London: Pickering and Linglis, 1961), p.85.
[4] K. Burger, "Prophets in the New Testament" in *The Schaff-Herzog Encyclopedia of Religious Knowledge*, 3 vols., (New York: Funk and Wagnalls, 1884), 3:1940.
[5] A. R. Faussett in Jamieson, Fausset, and Brown, eds., *Critical and Explanatory Commentary on the Bible*, 2 vols., (Hartford: Scranton, n.d.), 2:288.
[6] Ibid., 2:289.

Of 1 Corinthians 14:6 he writes: "revelation . . . prophesying — corresponding one to the other; 'revelation' being the supernatural unveiling of Divine truths to man, 'prophesying' the enunciation to men of such revelations."[7]

6. Francis Foulkes

Of the prophets in Ephesians 4:11 is understood thus by Foulkes:

> They stand out clearly from the New Testament as men of inspired utterance, whose ministry of the word was of the utmost importance for the young Church. . . . The ministry, or at least the name, of prophet also soon died out in the Church. Their work, receiving and declaring the Word of God under direct inspiration of the Spirit, was most vital before there was a canon of New Testament Scripture.[8]

7. H. M. Gwatkin

"The prophets ranked next to the apostles (1 Cor. 12:28; Eph. 4:11), and are even coupled with them (Eph. 2:20; 3:5) as receivers and layers of foundations. . . ."[9]

8. S. M. Jackson and George W. Gilmore

> The Lord himself announced that after his death prophets would arise, men who in the same way and with the same authority as the messengers of God in the Old Testament would present the truths of approaching salvation to the people of Israel and urge them to decide either for or against them (Matt. 23:34; cf. Luke 11:49). . . . New Testament prophecy belongs to the period of the founding of the Church when faith especially needed the guidance and support of the spirit of Christ, and when the written Word either did not yet exist or was not in general use.[10]

---

[7] Ibid.

[8] Francis Foulkes, *Ephesians* in *Tyndale New Testament Commentaries* (Grand Rapids: Wm. B. Eerdmans, 1956), pp. 118-119.

[9] H. M. Gwatkin, "Prophets" in James Hastings, ed., *A Dictionary of the Bible*, 4 vols., (Edinburgh: T & T Clark, 1902), 4:128.

[10] S. M. Jackson and George W. Gilmore, eds., *The New Schaff-Herzog Encyclopedia of Religious Knowledge*, (NY: Funk and Wagnalls, 1911), 9:277.

9. George Eldon Ladd

> Coupled with apostles were prophets (Eph. 2:20; 3:5), who were men endowed by the Holy Spirit sometimes to prophesy future events (Acts 11:28; 21:10) but more often to speak words of revelation for the edification of the church (1 Cor. 14:6, 29-30). The gifts of both apostleship and prophecy were given by the Holy Spirit (1 Cor. 14:4, 28; Eph. 4:11), and were not offices to which men could be elected by the church. The authority of both was spiritual and not appointive or official or legal. The apostles exercised an authority in ruling the churches that apparently was not exercised by the prophets. The authority of the latter was largely in the area of teaching.[11]

He continues later:

> It is obvious that apart from the priority of the apostles and prophets, Paul attaches no special order of importance to the several gifts. Apostles and prophets were of primary importance because they were the vehicles of revelation (Eph. 3:5) and thereby provided the foundation for the church (Eph. 2:20). All apostles were prophets but not all prophets were apostles. Apostles were commissioned with an authority in the churches that the prophets did not possess. Prophets spoke by direct illumination of the Spirit (the Word of God). We must remember that the early churches did not possess the New Testament Scriptures that preserve for successive generations the prophetic witness of the meaning of the person and work of Christ. We do not know, although we can assume, that they possessed a fixed body of catechetical tradition. In any case, it is clear from 1 Corinthians 12 and 14 that prophets were men inspired by the Spirit to speak in intelligible language a revelation from God. . . . Prophecy is the medium for disclosing the mysteries of God (1 Cor. 13:2).[12]

10. H. A. W. Meyer.

Of Romans 12:6, Meyer writes:

---

[11] George Eldon Ladd, *A Theology of the New Testament* (Grand Rapids: Wm. B. Eerdmans, 1974), pp. 535-536.

[12] Ibid., pp. 535-536.

> *Propheteia, the gift of theopneustic discourse*, which presupposes *apokalupsis*, and the form of which, appearing in different ways (hence also in the *plural* in 1 Cor. 13:8; 1 Thess. 5:20), was not ecstatic, like the speaking with tongues, but was an activity of the nous enlightened and filled with the consecration of the Spirit's power, disclosing hidden things, and profoundly seizing, chastening, elevating, carrying away men's hearts, held in peculiar esteem by the apostles (1 Cor. 14:1).[13]

Elsewhere he writes of 1 Corinthians 12:10:

> *Prophetic speech*, i.e. address flowing from revelation and impulse of the Holy Spirit, which without being bound for that matter to a particular office, suddenly (14:30) unveils the depth of the human heart (14:25) and of the divine counsels (3:10; Eph. 3:5), and thereby works with peculiar power for enlightenment, admonition, and comforting of the faithful (14:3), and so as to win over the unbelieving (14:24).[14]

11. Leon Morris

On 1 Corinthians 12:10 Morris writes: "*Prophecy* is inspired speech.... His point is that the Spirit gives to some the ability to utter inspired words, which convey the message of God to the hearers."[15]

Of 1 Corinthians 14:1 he observes: "But among the *gifts*, Paul gives the first place to prophecy.... It denotes something rather like our preaching, but it is not identical with it. It is not the delivery of a carefully prepared sermon, but the uttering of words directly inspired of God."[16]

---

[13] H. A. W. Meyer, *Critical and Exegetical Handbook to Romans* (New York: Funk and Wagnalls, 1889), p. 472.

[14] H. A. W. Meyer, *Critical and Exegetical Handbook to 1 Corinthians* (New York: Funk and Wagnalls, 1884), p. 282.

[15] Leon Morris, *1 Corinthians* in *Tyndale New Testament Commentaries* (Grand Rapids: Wm. B. Eerdmans, 1958), p. 172.

[16] Ibid., p. 177.

12. H. C. G. Moule

> In [Ephesians] 4:11, again, we have the "prophet" named *next to the "Apostle"* among the gifts of the glorified Saviour to this Church; a suggestion of the great prominence and importance of the function. We take the word here, then, to mean such "prophets" as Judas and Silas (Acts 15:32); men, we gather, who, though not of one office with the Apostles, shared some of their functions; were directly inspired, on occasion, with knowledge of the future (Acts 11:28), and with truth of spiritual doctrine (3:5, and 1 Cor. 14); and were specially commissioned to preach and teach such things revealed."[17]

Of Romans 12:6 he comments: "*prophecy,* inspired utterance, a power from above...."[18]

13. C. von Orelli

> According to the uniform teaching of the Bible the prophet is a *speaker* of or for God. His words are not the production of his own spirit, but come from a higher source.... [T]he contents of the prophecy have not originated in their own reflection or calculation; and just as little is this prophecy the product of their own feelings, fears, or hopes, but, as something extraneous to man and independent of him, it has with a Divine certainty entered the soul of the prophet.[19]

Later he points out regarding New Testament prophecy:

> *Prophecy in the NT.*... In the congregation the office of prophecy is again found, differing from the proclamation of the gospel by the apostles, evangelists, and teachers. In the NT the terms *prophetes, propheteia, propheteuo,* signify speaking under the extraordinary influence of the Holy Ghost. Thus in Acts 11:27f (prophecy of a famine by Agabus); 21:10f (prediction of the

---

[17] H. C. G. Moule, *Ephesians* (Grand Rapids: Kregal, 1893 [rep.]), pp. 83, 84.
[18] H. C. G. Moule, *The Epistle to the Romans* (Minneapolis: Klock and Klock, 1982 [rep.]), p. 331.
[19] C. von Orelli, in James Orr, ed., *The International Standard Bible Encyclopedia*, 4 vols., (Grand Rapids: Wm. B. Eerdmans, 1929 [rep. 1956]), 4:2459.

sufferings of Paul); 13:1f (exhortation to mission work); 21:9ff (prophetical gift of the daughters of Philip), Paul himself also had this gift (Acts 16:6ff; 18:9; 22:17ff; 27:37f). In the public services of the church, prophecy occupied a prominent position (see esp. 1 Cor. 14).[20]

14. Philip Schaff

In the Bible "prophecy" on the one hand includes more than the prediction of future events, it is a speaking *for* God not merely *beforehand*; on the other hand, it is not identical with preaching. In the New Testament the reference is to the gift of immediate inspiration, for the occasion, "leading the recipient to deliver, as the mouth of God, the particular communication which he had received" (Hodge).[21]

Of 1 Corinthians 12:10 he writes: *"prophecy* — uttering by inspiration the mind of God about things past, present, or future...."[22]

15. John R. W. Stott.

[W]e are to think of them [apostles and prophets] as inspired teachers, organs of divine revelation, bearers of divine authority.... New Testament prophets are meant. The church stands or falls by its loyal dependence on the foundation truths which God revealed to his apostles and prophets, and which are now preserved in the New Testament Scriptures.[23]

16. Milton S. Terry

Philippi (Commentary on Romans 12:6) observes that "the New Testament idea of the prophetic office is essentially identical with that of the Old Testament. Prophets are men who, inspired by the Spirit of God, and impelled to theopneustic discourse, partly remove the veil from the future (Rev. 1:3; 22:7,10; John 11:51;

---

[20] Ibid., 4:2464.
[21] Philip Schaff, *Epistles of St. Paul*, in Philip Schaff, ed., *Popular Commentary on the New Testament* (Edinburgh: T & T Clark, 1882), p. 126.
[22] Ibid., p. 209.
[23] John R. W. Stott, *God's New Society* (Downer's Grove: Inter-Varsity Press, 1979), p. 107.

Acts 11:27,28; 21:10,11. Comp. 1 Pet. 1:10) — partly make known concealed facts of the present, either in discovering the secret counsel and will of God (Luke 1:67; Acts 13:1; Eph. 3:5), or in disclosing the hidden thoughts of man (1 Cor. 14:24,25), and dragging into light his unknown deeds (Matt. 26:68; Mark 14:65; Luke 22:64; John 4:19) — partly dispense to their hearers instruction, comfort, exhortation, in animated, powerfully impassioned language, going far beyond the wonted limits of the capacity for teaching, which, although spiritual, still confines itself within the forms of reason (Matt. 7:28, 29; Luke 24:19 . . . 1 Cor. 14:3,4,31).[24]

17. *M. R. Vincent*

Regarding Romans 12:6 Vincent notes:

> In the New Testament, as in the Old, the prominent idea is not *prediction*, but the inspired delivery of warning, exhortation, instruction, judging, and making manifest the secrets of the heart. . . . The New-Testament prophets are distinguished from *teachers*, by speaking under direct divine inspiration.[25]

Regarding Paul's statement in 1 Corinthians 12:10 on "prophecies," Vincent observes that these are: "[U]tterances under immediate divine inspiration: delivering inspired exhortations, instructions, and warnings."[26]

18. *W. E. Vine*

Vine speaks of prophecy's function, as in 1 Corinthians 12:10: "Prophecy was not limited to foretelling the future, it consisted in a Divinely imparted power to tell forth the mind of God previous to the full revelation afterwards provided in the completed Scriptures."[27]

---

[24] Milton S. Terry, *Biblical Hermeneutics*, 2nd ed., (Grand Rapids: Zondervan, n.d. [rep. 1983]), pp. 406-407, n. 2.
[25] M. R. Vincent, *Word Studies in the New Testament*, 4 vols., *The Epistles of Paul* (Grand Rapids: Wm. B. Eerdmans, 1887 [1977]), 3:156.
[26] Ibid., 3:176.
[27] W. E. Vine, *1 Corinthians* (London: Oliphants, 1951), p. 169.

On verse 28 of the same text he writes: " — the ministry of the prophets in the assembly was by supernatural revelations, directly giving the mind of God for the occasion. . . . With the completion of the canon of Scripture prophets passed away. . . ."[28]

19. B. F. Westcott

Westcott writes on Ephesians 4:11: "The *prophetes* was an inspired teacher. . . . The prophets are frequently combined with the apostles as having peculiar authority. . . ."[29]

Conclusion

As stated previously, the weight given the citations above is secondary to that given to an exposition of Scripture. It must be recognized, however, that the citations above are from devout men noted for their love of Scripture and their understanding of it. Consequently, this survey should be helpful to any who consider the question from the historical evangelical perspective.

---

[28] Ibid., 3:176.
[29] B. F. Westcott, *St. Paul's Epistle to the Ephesians* (Grand Rapids: Wm. B. Eerdmans, 1950 [rep.]), p. 62.

7

A Survey of John Calvin's Writings

The Issue

In debate regarding the question of the nature and continuance of the gift of prophecy, reference is frequently made to the great reformer John Calvin. Calvin is deemed useful by Presbyterian charismatics primarily for the following two reasons:

First, the historical problem. At some places Calvin seems to hold to positions which allow the continuance of prophetic utterances in post-canon forming Christian history. *If* such is the case, then he provides evidence that there is and should be some degree of latitude among Reformed scholars on this question. Calvin would be a giant example of the historical acceptability of the continuance of charismatic phenomena.

Second, the theoretical problem. That being the case (it is asserted), a question naturally arises: Would confessional churches — such as the Presbyterian Church in America — then refuse to allow even John Calvin to enter their pastorate because of his views regarding the gift of prophecy? Surely the PCA and other Reformed churches holding to the Westminster Confession of Faith are not so dogmatic on this one issue as to be unwilling to tolerate John Calvin in its ministry!

In response to such an employment of Calvin, the presentation given below will provide: (1) Select statements from the writings of Calvin that appear supportive of the Presbyterian charismatic position regarding the gift of prophecy. (2) Pertinent observations on such an employment of Calvin, which effectively nullify such argumentation regarding the question of prophecy in the PCA and other churches and confessional bodies.

Before actually beginning this study, procedural comments need to be made. The editions of Calvin's works employed below — unless otherwise noted — are as follows:

> *Institutes of the Christian Religion*, ed. by John T. McNeill, Trans. by Ford Lewis Battles, in *The Library of Christian Classics*, Vols. 20 and 21 (Philadelphia: Westminster Press, 1965).
>
> *Calvin's New Testament Commentary: A New Translation*, ed. by David W. Torrance and Thomas F. Torrance (Grand Rapids: Wm. B. Eerdmans). (Various translators and dates according to particular volumes.)

Alleged Charismatic Statements from John Calvin

The following three statements found in Calvin's works are those that are most frequently deemed supportive of the charismatic Presbyterian's position. They will be cited first, then analyzed in another section of this study.

"Paul applies the name 'prophets' not to all those who were interpreters of God's will, but to those who excelled in a particular revelation (Eph. 4:11). This class either does not exist today or is less commonly seen."[1]

"It is not clear that he intended here [Rom. 12:6] only those wonderful graces by which Christ adorned His Gospel at the beginning. We see rather that he is referring simply to ordinary gifts which remain perpetually in the Church."[2]

"For it is difficult to make up one's mind about gifts and offices of which the Church has been deprived for so long, except for mere traces or shades of them, which are still to be found."[3]

---

[1] Calvin, *Institutes*, 4:3:4, 2:1057.
[2] Calvin, *Romans and Thessalonians*, p. 269.
[3] Calvin, *1 Corinthians*, p. 271. At 1 Cor. 12:28, while discussing "prophets."

Calvin, Prophecy, and Presbyterianism

We will now set forth several objections to the Presbyterian charismatic use of Calvin. Calvin should not be of much help to Presbyterian charismatics due to the following problems:

The Problem of Anachronism

Granting for the moment (merely for sake of argument) that Calvin's view of prophecy is that of the Presbyterian charismatic, the argument as employed is irrelevant due to its being anachronistic. That is, it must be kept in mind that Calvin lived over 400 years ago — 100 years prior, even, to the Westminster Assembly. Consequently, it must be noted that:

First, Calvin was at the very beginning of the Reformation and was rediscovering "lost" or obscured Biblical truths. As B. B. Warfield has commented: "We must bear in mind, on the one hand, that the young Calvin's book had practically no predecessors, but broke out a new path itself. . . ."[4]

Calvin cannot be "discredited" for not holding to all the truths of which the Westminster Divines were aware in their more advanced stage of the progress of reformational doctrine. Post-Westminster Reformed scholars hold to far different positions on this issue than that espoused by charismatics.

Second, Calvin never subscribed to the Westminster Standards and thus cannot be properly brought under confessional scrutiny, and judicially censored, as it were. We cannot judge as to whether or not Calvin's view would keep him out of a Presbyterian denomination such as the PCA. We do not know what his view would be today, after further reflection on the issues.

Third, furthermore, there is some confusion in Calvin's position, it would seem. *If* he does at one place sound as if

---

[4] B. B. Warfield, in John Allen, translator, John Calvin, *Institutes of the Christian Religion* [Philadelphia: Presbyterian Board of Christian Education, n.d.], p. xiv.

he holds to a view of prophecy similar to that with which we are concerned, it may be that contradictory positions espoused by Calvin in other places represent a later development of his thought. After all, he did do his writing over a period of several years and even edited his published writings from time to time.

The Problem of Uncertainty

Calvin himself admits to having difficulty understanding what the nature of the gift of prophecy was. At 1 Corinthians 12:28 after five paragraphs of discussion, he notes: "Should anyone be of a different opinion, I am willing to acknowledge that there is room for it, and will not pick a quarrel with him because of it. For it is difficult to make up one's mind about gifts and offices, of which the Church has been deprived for so long, except for mere traces or shades of them, which are still to be found."[5]

The Problem of Fundamental Distinctions

First, Calvin makes a distinction between the gift of prophecy which resided in the early church and the gift of prophecy that may reside in the church today. In some places, he sees the gifts and/or offices of the apostle and the prophet as temporary only. This would make his position different in a most important respect from the charismatic view. This would effectively render appeal to Calvin on this matter useless.

For instance, on Romans 12:6 he writes: "It is not clear that he intended here only those wonderful graces by which Christ adorned His Gospel at the beginning. We see rather that he is referring simply to ordinary gifts which remain perpetually in the Church."[6]

Of Ephesians 4:11 he comments: "It should be observed, also, that, of the offices which Paul enumerates, only the last two [pastor and teacher] are perpetual. For God adorned

---

[5] Calvin, *1 Corinthians*, p. 271.
[6] Calvin, *Romans and 1 Thessalonians*, p. 269.

His Church with apostles, evangelists and prophets, only for a time, except that where religion has broken down, He raises up evangelists apart from Church order, to restore the pure doctrine to its lost position. But without pastors and doctors there can be no government of the Church."[7]

In his commentary at 1 Corinthians 12:28 he writes: "As far as the verse before us is concerned, we must note that some of the offices, to which Paul is referring, are permanent, while others are temporary. The permanent offices are those which are necessary for the government of the Church. The temporary ones, on the other hand, are those which were designed, at the beginning, for the founding of the Church, and the setting up of the Kingdom of Christ; and which ceased to exist after a while."[8]

Second, Calvin specifically denies what Presbyterian charismatics affirm at one critical juncture of the debate: Calvin denies that the gift of prophecy in Romans, 1 Corinthians, and 1 Thessalonians — and even some places in Acts — may include the predictive element. For Calvin, predictive prophecy has ceased. On Romans 12:6 he writes in this regard:

> Some interpreters mean by *prophecy* the power of predicting, which flourished in the Church about the time when the Gospel began, as the Lord was at that time desirous to commend the dignity and excellence of His kingdom by every means. . . . I prefer, however, to follow those who understand the word in a wider sense to mean the peculiar gift of revelation by which a man performs the office of interpreter with skill and dexterity in expounding the will of God. In the Christian Church, therefore, prophecy at the present day is simply the right understanding of Scripture and the particular gift of expounding it, since all the ancient prophecies and all the oracles of God have been concluded in Christ and His Gospel. Paul understood it in this sense when he said, "I would have you all speak with tongues, but rather that ye should prophesy" (1 Cor. 14:5), and "We know in part and we prophesy in part" (1 Cor. 13:9). It is not clear that he intended

---

[7] Calvin, *Ephesians*, pp. 179-180.
[8] Calvin, *1 Corinthians*, p. 270.

here to consider only those wonderful graces by which Christ adorned His Gospel at the beginning. We see rather that he is referring simply to ordinary gifts which remain perpetually in the Church.[9]

On 1 Thessalonians 5:20 Calvin comments: "By the term prophesying, however, I do not mean the gift of foretelling the future, but as in 1 Cor. 14:3, the science of the interpretation of Scripture.... In the present passage, therefore, let us understand prophesying to mean the interpretation of Scripture applied to present need."[10]

He writes regarding 1 Corinthians 12:28: "I am certain, in my own mind, that he means by prophets, not those endowed with the gift of foretelling, but those who were blessed with the unique gift of dealing with Scripture.... My reason for thinking so is that Paul prefers prophecy to all other gifts, because it is a greater source of edification, a statement that can hardly be made to apply to the prediction of future events."[11]

On Acts 21:9 Calvin notes:

> But God wished to give lustre to the beginnings of the Gospel by this method of raising up men and women to predict coming events. For very many years now prophecies had almost ceased among the Jews, so that their minds might be more attentive or more alert to hear the new voice of the Gospel. Therefore when prophecy returned, as if by restoration, it was a sign of a more complete situation. Yet the reason why it ceased a little later, appears to have been the same. For God sustained the people of old by various predictions until, by His advent, Christ put an end to all prophecies. Therefore it was fitting for the new reign of Christ to be distinguished and adorned in this way, so that all might know that the promised visitation of God was a present reality, and, on the other hand, it was proper for it to flourish only for a short time, so that believers might not always be in a state of uncertainty, or so that an opportunity might not be given to those of a curious turn of mind to be looking repeatedly for, or devising, something new.

---

[9] Calvin, *Romans and 1 Thessalonians*, p. 268-269.
[10] Ibid., p. 376-377.
[11] Calvin, *1 Corinthians*, p. 271.

> For we know that, when that power had already been taken away, there were, nevertheless, many fanatics who boasted that they were prophets. And it is also possible that the perverseness of men deprived the Church of this gift. But this one reason ought to be sufficient, that, by taking away prophecies, God bore witness that their end and fulfillment were present in Christ.[12]

The Problem of Confessional Contradiction

In some places in Calvin's writings, it seems that he expresses views that are clearly and fundamentally out of accord with the Westminster Standards and other PCA governmental documents. These views, if held by men seeking pastorates in the PCA, would surely preclude their acceptance into the PCA.

In his *Institutes* at 4:3:4 he writes:

> Those who preside over the government of the church in accordance with Christ's institution are called by Paul as follows: first apostles, then prophets, thirdly evangelists, fourthly pastors, and finally teachers (Eph. 4:11). Of these only the last two have an ordinary office in the church; the Lord raised up the first three at the beginning of his Kingdom, and now and again revives them as the need of the times demands.[13]

On the next page he comments: "Still, I do not deny that the Lord has sometimes at a later period raised up apostles, or at least evangelists in their place, as has happened in our own day."[14] He goes on to state: "Paul applies the name 'prophets' not to all those who were interpreters of God's will, but to all those who excelled in a particular revelation. This class either does not exist today or is less commonly seen."[15]

---

[12] Calvin, *Acts*, pp. 194-195.

[13] Calvin, *Institutes*, p. 1056.

[14] Ibid., p. 1057. In a footnote, the editor comments that Calvin's references to "apostles" in his own day was "referring chiefly to Luther, whom he elsewhere often praises. Cf. Calvin's *Defensio adversus Pighium*, where Luther is called 'a distinguished apostle of Christ by whose ministry the light of the gospel has shone.'"

[15] Ibid.

The following quotations pose a difficulty only if Calvin deems such still to be resident in the church. After observing the continuance of the "prophets" in the church, he often speaks of their revelatory function:"The prophetic office was more eminent on account of the singular gift of revelation in which they excelled."[16] Elsewhere he states: "I take the term *prophecy* to mean that unique and outstanding gift of revealing what is the secret will of God, so that the prophet is, so to speak, God's messenger to men."[17] Still again:

> I bracket revelation and prophesying together, and I think that prophesying is the servant of revelation. I take the same view about knowledge and teaching. Therefore whatever anyone has obtained by revelation he gives out in prophesying. Teaching is the way to pass on knowledge. So a prophet will be the interpreter and minister of revelation. This supports, rather than conflicts with, the definition of prophecy which I gave earlier. For I said that prophesying does not consist in the simple or bare interpretation of Scripture, but also includes the knowledge for making it apply to the needs of the hour, and that can only be obtained by revelation and the special influence of God.[18]

At 1 Corinthians 14:37 Calvin writes:

> He shows even more confidence in saying immediately afterwards, if any man is ignorant, let him be ignorant. This was certainly legitimate in Paul's case, for he had no doubt at all in his own mind about the revelation he had received from God; and also, he ought to have been well known to the Corinthians, so that they should have regarded him as an apostle of the Lord, and in no other way. But everyone cannot make such a claim for himself; or, if he does do so, people will only laugh at him, and quite rightly, for showing off; for there is room for confidence like Paul's only when the words that are on the lips of men are borne out by facts. Paul was stating no more than the truth in saying that his injunctions were those of the Lord; many, on the other hand, will allege the same thing without any warrant. The whole thing hinges on

---

[16] Calvin, *Institutes*, 4:3:5 (p. 1058).
[17] Calvin, *1 Corinthians*, p. 263 (at 12:10).
[18] Ibid., p. 288 (at 14:6).

the fact that it is clear that a man is speaking by the Holy Spirit, and is not expressing his own ideas, when he cannot bear to be called to order. But the man who is a genuine instrument of the Holy Spirit, and nothing else, will, like Paul, dare to make the confident assertion that those who will reject his teaching are not prophets or spiritual people.[19]

Conclusion

It would seem clear from the above considerations that Presbyterian charismatics should not be able to convincingly employ Calvin in their defense. Of course, this is not to disparage Calvin's genuine contribution to Reformed theology; Calvin stands without peer in terms of stature and influence. But if Calvin is being properly understood by the charismatics, he stands very much in the minority as a noteworthy Reformed theologian who seems even remotely supportive of the charismatic view of the gift of prophecy and its currency in the Church today.

---

[19] Ibid., p. 308.

Part III
ECCLESIASTICAL QUESTIONS

8

The Westminster Confession of Faith

It should go without saying that to conservative Presbyterians the highest governmental document (under the Scripture, of course) is the venerable Westminster Standards — including the Confession of Faith and the Larger and Shorter Catechisms. Thus, ministers, elders, and deacons in conservative Presbyterian denominations take solemn vows stating their commitment to the system of doctrine contained in the Westminster Standards.

It is often the case that Presbyterian charismatics have even appealed to the Westminster Standards for support. They have argued that their position regarding the continuance of prophecy in the Church is supported by — or at least tolerated in — these documents. A careful study of relevant passages from these documents, however, should convince the objective reader of the futility of such.

Westminster Confession of Faith 1:1

Although the light of nature, and the works of creation and providence do so far manifest the goodness, wisdom, and power of God, as to leave men inexcusable; yet are they not sufficient to give that knowledge of God, and of His will, which is necessary unto salvation. Therefore it pleased the Lord, at sundry times, and in divers manners, to reveal Himself, and to declare that His will unto His Church; and afterwards, for the better propagating of the truth, and for the more sure establishment and comfort of the Church against the corruption of the flesh, and the malice of Satan and of the world, to commit the same wholly unto writing: which maketh the Holy Scripture to be most necessary; those former ways of God's revealing His will unto His people being now ceased.

This statement clearly states that the "former ways of God's revealing His will unto His people" are "*now ceased.*" Presbyterian charismatics, however, insist that this phrase refers only to redemptive-historical revelation, and not to "lower" forms of verbal, divine revelation. Such "lower planed" revelation does not, they aver, establish doctrinal truth or contradict Scripture, even though it is the voice of the Living God. It is given by God for personal and limited direction, as in a warning of impending disaster, the giving of "non-binding" personal direction, and the like. Thus, it should be tolerated within confessional Presbyterian circles.

Understanding WCF 1:1

Despite charismatic objections, this closing phrase teaches that *all* means by which God verbally or visually communicated with His people in the canon forming era of redemptive history have ceased. Note:

The Phrase is Comprehensive

The closing statement is comprehensive, and not limited solely to the making known of the doctrinal-redemptive truths relative to salvation. It is true that the first paragraph does speak of doctrinal-redemptive truth. The Westminster Divines, however, ended that paragraph by making a strong statement which would cover not only the preceding, but the following statements — many of which go beyond the focus on redemption.

The intent of this chapter in the Confession is not to deal solely with redemptive truths, there are other chapters later that do that. The design of this chapter is to deal with divine authority — an authority found exclusively in Scripture. Paragraph 1 speaks of two modes of revelation: natural revelation to all men and verbal revelation to His people. When it closes it distinctly says "the former ways of God's revealing His will unto His people (are) now ceased." This was added in explanation as to why God committed His Word to writing.

A cursory check of Scripture demonstrates that God revealed His will by dreams, visions, prophecy, word, and so forth. These are now ceased, according to the Confessional position. Of course, it is logically the case by "good and necessary consequence" that if all God's ways of revealing His will are ceased, then it holds that there will be (among other things) no more doctrinal-redemptive truth.

The Phrase Covers All of "Faith and Life"

In keeping with the thrust of the first chapter, the Westminster Divines make the following declaration regarding the sixty-six canonical books in paragraph 2: "All which are given by inspiration of God to be the rule of *faith* and *life*." Alluded to here are not just doctrinal-redemptive matters (i.e., matters of "*faith*"), but also matters of all of "*life*."

We do not need another voice from God; He has given us His Word to direct us in life. We show our faith and trust in walking by faith, not by sight. The Word of God, according to Reformed teaching, is wholly sufficient for our needs. We do not today need a new "word of prophecy" for "edification." We have the Bible which perfectly equips us for every good work and for growth in grace (2 Tim. 3:16-17; Heb. 5:12-14; 1 Pet. 2:2).

In the same vein we read in paragraph 6: "The whole counsel of God concerning *all things* necessary for His own glory, man's salvation, faith and *life*, is either expressly set down in Scripture, or by good and necessary consequence may be deduced from Scripture: unto which *nothing* at any time is to be added, whether by new revelations of the Spirit, or traditions of men."

In this paragraph the Scripture is protected against two extremes. On the one hand, it is protected from a Roman Catholic-like authority of "tradition." On the other hand, it is protected from the mystics who claim "new revelations of the Spirit." Consequently, it militates against the charismatic view.

The Holy Spirit Speaks In Scripture

We do not need "prophets"[1] to interpret Scripture for us today, for "the infallible rule of interpretation of Scripture is the Scripture itself; and therefore, when there is a question about the true and full sense of any Scripture (which is not manifold, but one), it must be searched and known by other places that speak more clearly" (WCF 1:9). Thus, in WCF 1:10 we are taught that "the supreme judge by which all controversies of religion are to be determined, and all decrees of councils, opinions of ancient writers, doctrines of men, and private spirits, are to be examined, and in whose sentence we are to rest, can be no other but the Holy Spirit speaking in Scripture." Here there is not the least inkling that the Holy Spirit could audibly speak to us to clarify the meaning of His Word. In controversy we often refer to councils, ancient writers, doctrines of men, and private spirits (i.e., personal convictions), but these must be weighed in the balance of Scripture as to their validity. We are not to expect the audible voice of God to assist us in this.

The Divines Taught Prophecy Ceased

That the Westminster Divines understood the gift of prophecy as having ceased (as per the teaching of WCF 1:1) is clear upon the following considerations:

First, the original Westminster Assembly not only formulated and passed the Confession of Faith, Larger and Shorter Catechisms, but also The Form of Government. The heading of the original Form of Government reads as follows: "The Form of Presbyterial Church-Government and of Ordination of Ministers; Agreed upon by the Assembly

---

[1] By "prophets" we are here referring to prophets in the biblical sense, not the ecclesiastical sense. Today many use the term "prophet" to speak of the role of the preacher. This usage is not found in Scripture. See citation from John Brown (entry number 8) in Chapter 5 above.

of Divines at Westminster, with the assistance of commissioners from the Church of Scotland."

In its third section entitled "Of the Officers of the Church" we find the following statement: "The officers which Christ hath appointed for the edification of his church, and the perfecting of the saints, are some extraordinary, as apostles, evangelists, and prophets, which are ceased."

Clearly, the Westminster Divines viewed the prophets of the Apostolic Church as being extraordinary and temporary. Surely their views in this section of their labors must be considered to be consistent with their views expressed elsewhere.

Second, research in the writings of the Westminster Divines indicates that we must understand the Westminster Standards as teaching the cessation of the gift and office of prophecy. B. B. Warfield provides for us some helpful statements from a couple of the Westminster Divines. He cites Edward Reynolds, one of the commissioners to the Westminster Assembly:

> It is the spirit of wisdom and revelation, which both openeth the heart to the word, giving an understanding to know the scriptures, and openeth the scriptures to the heart; for he takes of Christ's, and sheweth it unto us. . . . The spirit doth not reveal truth unto us, as he did in the primitive patefaction thereof to the prophets and apostles, — by divine and immediate inspiration. . . .[2]

Later he quotes John Lightfoot, another divine:

> Now was the whole will of God revealed and committed to writing, and from henceforth must vision, and prophecy, and inspiration, cease for ever.
> How may Christians inquire of God in their doubtings, as Israel did, here and elsewhere, in theirs? I must answer briefly, and that in the words of God himself, "To the law and to the testament"; to

---

[2] Benjamin B. Warfield, *The Westminster Assembly and Its Work* (Cherry Hill, NJ: Mack, n.d. [rep. 1972]), p. 232.

the written Word of God, "Search the Scriptures." As you might appeal to Balaam to bear witness concerning the blessedness of Israel, whereas he was called forth to curse them; — so, for the proof of this matter, — viz. that there is now no other way to inquire of God, but only from his Word, — you may appeal to those very Scriptures, that they produce, that would maintain that there are revelations and inspirations still, and that God doth still very often answer his people by them. . . . To speak fully to this matter, I should declare this, — I. That, after God had completed and signed the Scripture-canons, Christians must expect revelations no more. . . . .. II. I should show, that the Scripture containeth all things necessary for us to know or to inquire of God about.

There is no promise in Scripture, whereupon the spirit of revelation is to be expected after the fall of Jerusalem. . . . At the fall of Jerusalem, all Scripture was written, and God's full will revealed; so that there was no farther need of prophecy and revelation. . . . IV. The standing ministry is the ordinary method, that God hath used for the instruction of his church.[3]

Conclusion

Clearly the theology of the Confession and of the divines is antithetical to continuing prophecy. Just as clearly the commitments of Confessionally based churches should be contrary to charismatic leanings. To ignore the confessional directives is not only dishonest (since church officers publicly claim to uphold them), but is immoral (since church officers vow before God and His Church to uphold them). In addition, it is practically dangerous, for while allowing the erosion of confessional integrity, it opens the church to neglect its doctrine in favor of potentially harmful, subjectivistic emotionalism.

---

[3] Ibid., p. 280ff.

9

The Presbyterian Church in America

The Book of Church Order

Under the New Testament, our Lord at first collected His people out of different nations, and united them to the household of faith by the ministry of extraordinary officers who received extraordinary gifts of the Spirit and who were agents by whom God completed His revelation to His church. Such officers and gifts related to new revelation have no successors since God completed His revelation at the conclusion of the Apostolic Age (*BCO* 7-1).

The ordinary and perpetual classes of office in the Church are Elders and Deacons. . . . (*BCO* 7-2a)

All Extraordinary Officers Have Ceased

The *BCO* speaks in the plural of "extraordinary officers" who received "revelation." Note, first, that admittedly it does not enumerate or specify the officers. But its historical background is the Westminster Form of Government. As shown above, the Form of Government did enumerate them and included among them the "prophet."

Second, with the reference in the plural we are left to determine which officers it speaks about. All are agreed that the apostle was established as an office. The only other possible extraordinary offices were those of "prophet" and "evangelist." And at least one of these is necessary to make the plural "officers" meaningful.

There Are Only Two Offices in the Church

The *BCO* allows for only two offices in the church: elder (both teaching and ruling) and deacon: "The officers of the Church, by whom all its powers are administered, are, according to the Scriptures, Teaching and Ruling Elders and Deacons" (*BCO* 1:4). These offices are dealt with in great detail in the *BCO*. These offices are understood to be the perpetual offices in the ongoing church, despite the prominence of prophets in the apostolic Church.

There Is No Allowance for Continued Prophecy

Nowhere in the *BCO* — either in the Form of Government or the Worship Directory — is there any mention of the office of prophet or the gift of prophecy, or even the possibility of either. The office of prophet was very much a public office involved in the worship of the apostolic Church (1 Cor. 14). Its omission in the *Book of Church Order* is silent evidence of its disallowance in the governing documents of the Presbyterian Church in America. Obviously, the office of "prophet" is considered to have ceased with the New Testament era."

Neither is there any mention of the minister's being gifted with the "gift of prophecy" in the *BCO* (see: *BCO* 8-4,5; 53-3). Nor is there mention of prophecy operative in the church as an aspect of worship (see: *BCO* 47-55), despite its being very prominent in the apostolic church. This is no mere oversight in the *Book of Church Order*, which is a very biblical document that was carefully developed.

The BCO Has Constitutional Authority

The *BCO* has constitutional authority for the PCA ministry. Hence, it may be used in ecclesiastical debate to clarify the PCA position on certain matters. That such is the case is obvious in light of the following: First, in the *BCO* Preface, paragraph III we have the PCA constitution defined:

> The Constitution of the Presbyterian Church in America consists of its doctrinal standards set forth in the Westminster Confession of Faith, together with the Larger and Shorter Catechisms the Book of Church Order, as adopted by the Church. (Cp. also: BCO 26-1)

Second, the General Assembly — the highest court of the church — stated in its Thirteenth General Assembly:

> When an exception to the *BCO* is dealing with a matter spoken to in the Westminster Confession of Faith and Catechisms of this church, the exception shall be dealt with as an exception to the Westminster Confession of Faith or Catechisms of this church. . . .
>
> Further, when an exception to the *BCO* is dealing with a matter that is itself one of the "general principles of Biblical polity," the exception shall be dealt with as the presbytery deals with an exception to the Westminster Confession of Faith or Catechisms. . . .[1]

General Assembly Actions

The Second General Assembly Pastoral Letter

The Second General Assembly "Pastoral Letter Concerning the Experience of the Holy Spirit in the Church Today" states: "[M]iracles related to revelation have ceased, since revelation was completed with the closing of the Canon in the New Testament era."[2]

This declaration of the Assembly is admittedly just a broad outline of that which is intolerable in terms of Presbyterian polity. It has its weakness in being overly broad. Nevertheless, despite this weakness it does specifically forbid any continuing "revelation."

"Bogue v. Ascension"

The Eighth General Assembly "Bogue v. Ascension Presbytery" judicial commission stated that:

> The Commission judges that the Presbytery failed in allowing questions about continuing revelation by Mr. [X] to remain unclarified in the examination, so that the fundamental teaching of

---

[1] *Minutes of the Thirteenth General Assembly of the Presbyterian Church in America* (St. Louis, MO: 1985), p. 107.

[2] *Minutes of the Second General Assembly of the Presbyterian Church in America*, (Macon, GA: 1974), p. 171ff ("Appendix").

the WCF and the *BCO* concerning the sufficiency and finality of revelation in Scripture was not adequately protected. The Commission judges that simply affirming that the canon is closed, and that supposed new revelations from God add nothing to the deposit of truth already found in Scripture does not cover all the negations concerning continuing revelation from God found in WCF 1:1,6 and *BCO* 7-1. These statements of the standards also negate the idea any extraordinary ways still continue in addition to Scripture as ways by which God verbally uncovers His will to His people. According to the testimony of complainants and respondents, Mr. [X] affirmed belief in extraordinary revelation by tongues interpreted, while at the same time affirming that such revelation from God was not to be added to the canon of Scripture.[3]

The decision declared that even the *affirming*, not just the *practicing* of such a theological position, is impermissible: "[In a particular] trial for ordination before the Presbytery, while indicating that he himself was not practicing the matter under discussion, [the prospective minister] (a) affirmed his belief. . . ."[4]

"Gentry v. Calvary Presbytery"

In a judicial case initiated by the present author, along with several other PCA elders, a complaint was filed against his presbytery's acceptance (by a split vote of 41-39) of a minister who held that the gift of prophecy continued in the church today. That minister held, further, that God could and does speak by audible voice to His people and that He could raise up prophets of the order of Agabus to prophesy future events.

The General Assembly accepted the judicial decision rendered by the judicial committee, which supported the complainants in the charge against presbytery's action. A portion of that decision read:

---

[3] *Minutes of the Eighth General Assembly of the Presbyterian Church in America* (Savannah, GA: 1980), p. 93.
[4] Ibid.

The *Westminster Confession of Faith* states in Chapter I Section I, "those former ways of God's revealing His will unto His people being now ceased." This closing statement is very strong and teaches that all means by which God verbally communicated with His people have ceased. the text appealed to is Hebrews 1:1,2. Thus Scripture would teach us that those ways by which God formerly revealed His will by dreams, visions, prophecy, voice, etc. are now ceased.

The *Westminster Confession of Faith* I:VI does not teach and should not be construed as allowing for continuing revelation, but sets forth the sufficiency of Scripture. Thus this section may not be appealed to in order to support the notion of continuing revelation. That in which we are to rest is none other than the Holy Spirit speaking in Scripture, WCF I:X, *Book of Church Order* 7-1. . . .

The Constitutional Standards of the PCA do not allow for a type of continuing revelation that is not canonical Scripture (which is complete) but is more than mere illumination and providence; a type of non-authoritative, non-canonical, new revelation.[5]

Some Confusion in the Documents

Despite all the official evidence above, which is contrary to the continuance of prophecy in the Church today, the Sixteenth General Assembly resolved two cases in such a way as to allow one to contradict (apparently) the other. This is a serious issue, which will require care in the future to either rectify the discrepancy, or at least to check its erosive power in the governing documents and actions of the PCA.

In the Sixteenth General Assembly's Case #10, *Serio against Palmetto Presbytery*, the judicial commission drew upon the actions of *Bogue v. Ascension Presbytery* and *Gentry v. Calvary Presbytery* to support the complainant. A portion of the decision rendered reads:

> The Constitutional Standards of the PCA do not allow for a type of continuing revelation that is not canonical Scripture (which is

---

[5] *Minutes of the Fourteenth General Assembly of the Presbyterian Church in America* (Philadelphia, PA: 1986), p. 229-230.

> complete) but is more than mere illumination and providence; a type of non-authoritative, non-canonical, new revelation.
>
> The view that maintains that such special revelation continues today strikes at the fundamental doctrine of the perfection and sufficiency of Holy Scripture.[6]

Its reliance upon and conformity with the earlier judicial decisions cited above is evident by its documentation, as well as its very language. But a contradictory decision was rendered in the same assembly. That complaint, *Rayburn v. Missouri Presbytery*, was not sustained, despite its following the same lines of argument and even employing the judicial decisions mentioned above.[7]

Conclusion

There is a small degree of confusion in the governing documents of the Presbyterian Church in America on the matter of the charismatic gift of prophecy. The two seemingly weaker statements are either overly broad (*Pastoral Letter*) or admittedly contradictory to a host of other statements (*Rayburn*). Nevertheless, the several specific statements prohibiting charismatic prophecy are strong and well-argued. These fit well within the confines of historic Reformed thought and the specific biblical exegesis mentioned above.

---

[6] *Sixteenth General Assembly of the Presbyterian Church in America* (Knoxville, TN:1988), p. 196.

[7] Ibid., pp. 213-214.

Part IV
THEOLOGICAL QUESTIONS

10

The Problem of the "Open Canon"

The Alleged Problem

Despite all the evidence presented heretofore, it has been asserted by some Presbyterian charismatics that a serious potential problem arises if our view is adopted. They argue that if we hold that *all* direct, verbal communication from God is "revelational" in the sense of the Westminster prohibition of continuing revelation, then we have dangerously allowed for the possibility of an "open canon." That is, if we believe such, we must accept the possibility that some lost revelatory communication from God given during the era of the formulation of the canon may yet be discovered. In light of our view, it is alleged, we would have to add it to our present canon. Such a position would be confessionally intolerable. The Church would always stand in expectation of the possibility of adding to the canon of Scripture. She would not be convinced of her possession of a whole revelation from God, for Scripture would be, at least potentially, incomplete.

Were the implications of this argument to follow logically, this would be an argument of genuine consequence. That such an argument is not as weighty as it might first appear, however, may be seen in the following citations from noted conservative and confessional Presbyterian and Reformed scholars. All the various implications of the argument will not be pursued, in that it would take us far afield of our present concern. The citation of the following scholars should, however, demonstrate the "problem" is an apparent, not a real problem at all.

Scholarly Observations

Charles Hodge, in essence, considered this very question over a century ago. In his consideration, which was not related to the charismatic angle, he defended a complete canon, despite the possibility of lost inspired writings.

> By the completeness of Scripture is meant that they contain all the extant revelations of God designed to be a rule of faith and practice to the Church. It is not denied that God reveals himself, even his eternal power and Godhead, by his works, and has done so from the beginning of the world. But all the truths thus revealed are clearly made known in his written Word. *Nor is it denied that there may have been, and probably were, books written by inspired men, which are no longer in existence. Much less is it denied that Christ and his Apostles delivered many discourses which were not recorded, and which, could they now be known and authenticated, would be of equal authority with the books now regarded as canonical.* All the Protestants insist upon is, that the Bible contains all the extant revelations of God, which he designed to be the rule of faith and practice for his Church.[1]

The very providence and grace of God are important considerations here. As Hodge notes, "the Bible contains all the extant revelations of God, *which he designed* [by His grace and through His providence, we might add] to be the rule of faith and practice for His Church." Surely no Christian would deny that *everything* Jesus spoke was inspired, inerrant revelation from God! And just as surely should no Christian forget that we do not have a record of everything that He taught while upon earth (John 21:25; Acts 1:1-3), nor even of all that the inspired apostles taught (Acts 2:40; 15:32).

Noted Reformed contender for the faith, J. Gresham Machen has written in this regard:

---

[1] Charles Hodge, *Systematic Theology*, 3 vols., (Grand Rapids: Wm. B. Eerdmans, 1871 [rep. 1973]), 1:182-183.

> But why should we not obtain information, in addition to that recorded in the Bible, about supernatural revelation given, indeed, not later but in Bible times? Well, it is perfectly conceivable that we might do so. It is perfectly conceivable, for example, that there might turn up in Egypt bits of papyrus affording true information about words of Jesus not contained in the four Gospels. But the bits of papyrus which have actually turned up so far hardly seem to provide such information. . . . On the whole, speaking broadly, we can certainly say that *all the supernatural revelation that we can be certain about, although no doubt other supernatural revelation was given in Bible times, is recorded in the pages of one book, the Bible.*[2]

Contemporary Reformed theologian R. Laird Harris continues in the same vein:

> Were all of the prophetic writings preserved? Of course we cannot say. Most of these inspired speeches of the prophets have perished. A number of their inspired writings may also have been lost. In the vicissitudes of his prison experiences, a number of Jeremiah's works, for example, may have been destroyed by enemies or lost by accident. Some of his writings may have been so strictly applicable to the siege of Jerusalem alone that he made no effort to preserve them. But the writings that we have were providentially preserved from destruction. *We may therefore add to our tests for canonicity the factor of divine providence in preserving for us such writings as God wished us to have through succeeding generations.* We have no knowledge of a sifting of a prophet's work by his contemporaries or successors. It was not that people chose what they wished to preserve. This would place the burden of forming a canon on uninspired people, rather than leaving it in the hands of God's inspired teachers.[3]

Notice of the role of providence in the preserving of necessary revelation should be made. Surely this factor is

---

[2] J. Gresham Machen, *The Christian Faith in the Modern World* (Grand Rapids: Wm. B. Eerdmans, 1947), p. 33.

[3] R. Laird Harris, *Inspiration and Canonicity of the Bible* (Grand Rapids: Zondervan, 1969), p. 175.

indisputably set against the Presbyterian charismatic claim of the danger of an open canon.

Another present-day contender for the orthodox, Reformed faith is Morton H. Smith, formerly the Stated Clerk of the Presbyterian Church in America for fifteen years, and presently Professor of Systematic Theology at Greenville Presbyterian Theological Seminary. His words are in perfect harmony with the views presented above.

> The most striking new feature of the revelation in this chapter is the fact that God addresses His rational creature in verbal revelation. We have already observed that verbal or spoken revelation accompanied the creative acts of God. Genesis 1:28,30 and 2:16,17 present the picture of God in direct personal communion with man, speaking to him, first of what He has given to him, and then of the probation connected with the tree of the knowledge of good and evil. *We may assume that, since this record serves only as a backdrop for understanding the fall, there may have been much more verbal communion between God and man in Eden that is not recorded for us. . . .*[4]

Conclusion

Though the theoretical danger of an open canon might appear at first to be valid as a philosophical argument, it can have no real merit as a theological argument. Such a philosophical argument must be considered in the light of God's revealed purpose and stated providential care for His people. *That* will comfort us to know that we are promised all that we have need of in terms of God's guiding Word.

We know, for instance, that there are some lost letters of Paul to the Corinthians: there was at least one in addition to the two we now possess in Scripture. This is clearly evidenced in 1 Corinthians 5:9-11.[5] Yet, Christians have for

---

[4] Morton H. Smith, *Systematic Theology: A Syllabus*, 3 vols. (Jackson, MS: Reformed Theological Seminary, 1974), 1:34.

[5] F. F. Bruce, *1 and 2 Corinthians* (New Century Bible Commentary), Matthew Black, ed., (Grand Rapids: Wm. B. Eerdmans, 1971), pp. 23-25; Donald B. Guthrie, *New Testament Introduction* (Downer's Grove, IL: Inter-Varsity Press, 1970 [1 vol. ed.]), pp. 425-439.

centuries recognized the completeness of God's revelation as contained in the sixty-six books of the Protestant canon.

The view of revelation presented in this book, which is an historically prominent view in orthodoxy and Reformed thought, does not open the door to the theoretical "open canon."

11

The Problem in the Book of Revelation

In addition to the alleged theological problem of the "open canon," which we considered in the last chapter, there is presumed to arise another problem with our view of prophecy when we approach the book of Revelation. Some Presbyterian charismatics have argued that Revelation 11 speaks of two future "prophets" who prophesy well after the close of the canon. Since the work of these prophets is held to be in the distant future, this presents a real problem for our view.

Those who argue in this way also note that miraculous signs accompany these prophets prophesying in the eschatological future, i.e. well beyond the era of the closing of the canon. Since the Book of Revelation allows that these prophets will prophesy in the future, it would seem that this is evidence that the gift of prophecy has not been withdrawn from the Church.

But again, this argument is not compelling on the following grounds (to name but a very few):

The Difficulty of Interpreting Revelation

The whole theological debate on the question of prophecy and continuing revelation must be founded upon the clear doctrinal and historical passages of Scripture. As a general rule of hermeneutics, it is widely recognized that the more clear and didactic portions of Scripture must cast their light on the symbolic-prophetic sections. It should go without saying that the proper interpretation of the book of Revelation is one of the most debated issues in all of exegetical studies. Any argument based on its prophecies would be inconclusive at best.

The Difficulty of the Book

The following noted Biblical scholars and commentators illustrate the extremely difficult nature of interpreting the Revelation. Their words of caution should not deter us from seeking to understand the Book of Revelation. But they should provide us with some cautious restraint, especially when a view we are presenting (e.g., the charismatic view of prophecy) is suspect on other grounds.

B. B. Warfield: "The boldness of [Revelation's] symbolism makes it the most difficult book of the Bible: it has always been the most variously understood, the most arbitrarily interpreted, the most exegetically tortured."[1]

Milton S. Terry: "No portion of the Holy Scripture has been the subject of so much controversy and of so many varying interpretations as the Apocalypse of John."[2]

Henry B. Swete: "To comment on this great prophecy is a harder task than to comment on a Gospel, and he who undertakes it exposes himself to the charge of presumption. I have been led to venture upon on what I know to be dangerous ground...."[3]

G. R. Beasley-Murray: "Revelation is probably the most disputed and difficult book in the New Testament."[4]

George Eldon Ladd: "Revelation is the most difficult of all New Testament books to interpret...."[5]

---

[1] B. B. Warfield, "The Book of Revelation" in Philip Schaff, ed., *A Religious Encyclopedia*, 3 vols., (NY: Funk and Wagnalls, 1883), 2:80.

[2] Milton S. Terry, *Biblical Hermeneutics* (Grand Rapids: Zondervan, n.d.), p. 466.

[3] Henry B. Swete, *Commentary on Revelation* (Grand Rapids: Kregal, 1906 [rep. 1977]), p. xii.

[4] G. R. Beasley-Murray, *The Book of Revelation*, in R. E. Clements and Matthew Black, eds., *New Century Bible* (London: Marshall, Morgan, and Scott, 1974), p. 5.

[5] George Eldon Ladd, *A Commentary on the Revelation of John* (Grand Rapids: Wm B. Eerdmans, 1972), p. 10.

Eduard Wilhelm Reuss: "Ideas of the Apocalypse are so widely different that a summary notice of the exegetical literature, mingling all together, would be inexpedient."[6]

Isbon T. Beckwith: "... no other book, whether in sacred or profane literature, has received in whole or in part so many different interpretations. Doubtless no other book has so perplexed biblical students throughout the Christian centuries down to our own times."[7]

The Difficulty of the Chapter

Besides the difficulty the book itself presents to the interpreter in general, Revelation 11 in particular — the very passage in question — is widely regarded as one of the more perplexing prophecies in the entire book. So not only is the propriety of bringing Revelation into the debate questionable, but the wisdom of using this particular portion of Revelation is also suspect. In this regard the following commentators may prove helpful.

Robert H. Mounce: "Most commentators note that chapter 11 is especially difficult to interpret."[8]

Albert Barnes: "The two witnesses, vers. 3-13. This is, in some respects, the most difficult portion of the book of Revelation, and its meaning can be stated only after a careful examination of the signification of the words and phrases used."[9]

---

[6] Eduard Wilhelm Reuss, *History of the Sacred Scriptures of the New Testament* (Edinburgh: T and T Clark, 1884), p. 155.

[7] John T. Beckwith, *The Apocalypse of John: Studies in Introduction* (Grand Rapids: Baker, 1919 [1967]), p. 1.

[8] Robert H. Mounce, *The Book of Revelation in The New International Commentary* (Grand Rapids: Wm. B. Eerdmans, 1977), p. 218.

[9] Albert Barnes, *Barnes' Notes on the New Testament* (Grand Rapids: Kregal, rep. 1983), p. 1642.

Problem in Revelation / 139

Herman Hoeksema: "Numerous are the answers given to the question as to the identity of these two witnesses. In fact, you can hardly conceive of a question with a greater variety of answers than this. All the ingenuity of man has sometimes been brought into play in order to find an answer to this question. Now it must undoubtedly be admitted that this is one of the most difficult questions in the Apocalypse...."[10]

Moses Stuart: "But who are these two witnesses? A question that has been the occasion, perhaps, of more conjecture and more unlimited speculation than almost any other which the Apocalypse has originated."[11]

Henry Alford: "No solution has ever been given to this portion of the prophecy."[12]

Adam Clarke: "This [chapter] is extremely obscure; the conjectures of interpreters are as unsatisfactory as they are endless on this point."[13]

W. Boyd Carpenter: "Such seems to be the general drift of this chapter. It is stated thus briefly and simply that it may be kept in mind as a leading idea in the comments which follow, and because the chapter is generally regarded as one of the most difficult in the book."[14]

Martin Kiddle: "Chap. xi. is at once the most difficult and the most important in the whole book of REVELATION."[15]

To use Revelation 11 as a biblical indication that the gift of prophecy has not be withdrawn from the Church, is not

---

[10] Herman Hoeksema, *Behold, He Cometh!* (Grand Rapids: Kregal, 1969), p. 374-375.
[11] Moses Stuart, *Commentary on the Apocalypse*, 2 vols., (Andover: Allen, Morrill, and Wardwell, 1845), 2:219.
[12] Henry Alford, "The Apocalypse of John" in *The Greek New Testament*, 4 vols., (Chicago: Moody, rep. 1958), Vol. 4, p. 658.
[13] Adam Clarke, *Clarke's Commentary*, 6 vols., (Nashville: Abingdon, rep., n.d.), 6:1005.
[14] W. Boyd Carpenter, "Revelation", in Charles John Ellicott, *Ellicott's Commentary on the Whole Bible*, 8 vols. (Grand Rapids: Zondervan, rep., n.d.), 8:584.
[15] Martin Kiddle, *The Revelation of St. John* (NY: Harper and Bros., 1940), p. 174.

a wise hermeneutical procedure. At best it can only be a supplementary argument.

Revelation 11 and the Futurist

If the reference in Revelation is to a yet future episode God's plan, then the comments of Reformed theologian Geerhardus Vos must be taken into account:

> The question may be raised, whether within the limits of the principles here laid down, there can be expected still further revelation entitled to a place in the scheme of N. T. Revelation. Unless we adopt the mystical standpoint, which cuts loose the subjective from the objective, the only proper answer to this question is, that new revelation can be added only, in case new objective events of a supernatural character take place, needing for their understanding a new body of interpretation supplied by God. This will actually be the case in the eschatological issue of things. What then occurs will constitute a new epoch in redemption worthy to be placed by the side of the great epochs in the Mosaic age and the age of the first Advent. Hence the Apocalypse mingles with the pictures of the final events transpiring the word of prophecy and of interpretation. We may say, then, that a third epoch of revelation is still outstanding. Strictly speaking, however, this will form less a group by itself than a consummation of the second group. It will belong to N.T. revelation as a final division. Mystical revelation claimed by many in the interim as a personal privilege is out of keeping with the genius of Biblical religion. Mysticism in this detached form is not specifically Christian.[16]

No orthodox theologian would deny that the Second Advent of Christ is a revelational event. In fact we should not doubt that it will involve an infallible, authoritative revelation of the justice of God. There may well be a new revelational outpouring of the Spirit in conjunction with this climactic act of revelation and history. But this says nothing about the interim. And the evidence from Scripture

---

[16] Geerhardus Vos, *Biblical Theology: Old and New Testaments* (Grand Rapids: Wm. B. Eerdmans, 1948), pp. 326f.

is that until at least the Coming of Christ revelation has ceased.

Revelation 11 and the Preterist

The "preterist" interpretation of the Book of Revelation, to which the present writer subscribes,[17] holds that the bulk of the Book of Revelation deals with events soon to occur from John's perspective (Rev. 1:1, 3, 19[Gk.]; 3:10; 6:10; 22:6,7, 12, 20).[18] It sees the theme of Revelation as dealing with God's divorce of Israel as His adulteress wife and Christ's taking of a new bride, the Church (Rev. 1:7[19]; 17; 21-22).

Because of the textually justified preteristic approach to Revelation, the preterist understands the prophetic episode in Revelation 11 as having *already occurred* in the era leading up to the destruction of the Temple in the first century. If the preterist view is correct, then this prophetic episode occurred *within* the very era when revelation was continuing and while the apostles were still living.

Though currently overshadowed by a more sensationalistic futurism, the preterist view of Revelation 11 has been held (and is still held) by many noted commentators and historians. Noted preterist interpreters include the following (listed in alphabetical order):

---

[17] See Kenneth L. Gentry, Jr. *The Beast of Revelation* (Tyler, TX: Institute for Christian Economics, 1989), ch. 2; Kenneth L. Gentry, Jr. *Before Jerusalem Fell: Dating the Book of Revelation* (Tyler, TX: Institute for Christian Economics, 1989), chs. 8-9; and Greg L. Bahnsen and Kenneth L. Gentry, Jr. *House Divided: The Break-up of Dispensational Theology* (Tyler, TX: Institute for Christian Economics, 1989), ch. 16.

[18] Compare also: Rom. 13:11,12; 16:20; 1 Cor. 7:26, 29-31; Col. 3:6; 1 Thess. 2:16; Heb. 10:25, 37; Jms. 5:8, 9; 1 Pet. 4:5, 7; 1 John 2:17, 18.

[19] That Israel is being referred to in Rev. 1:7, the theme verse, is evident in that it speaks of: (1) "the tribes" (cp. Rev. 5:5; 7:4-8; Acts 26:6,7), (2) the tribes in "the Land" (literally, cp. Rev. 7:1,2; Matt. 2:6,20; 27:45; Mark 15:33; Luke 4:25; 21:23; John 3:22; Rom. 9:27-28; Jms. 5:17), and (3) judgment coming upon "those who pierced him" (i.e., Israel, Matt. 23:34-36; Acts 2:22-23, 36; 3:13-15; 77:52; 1 Thess. 2:14-15).

Jay E. Adams (1966) B. W. Henderson (1903)
Greg L. Bahnsen (1980) John Peter Lange (1874)
David Chilton (1985) Francis Nigel Lee (1984)
Adam Clarke (1820) J. B. Lightfoot (1898)
Friedrich Dusterdieck (1852) Philip Schaff (1895)
George Edmundson (1913) Milton S. Terry (1895)
F. W. Farrar (1884) Cornelius Vanderwaal (1980)
James Hastings (1904)

Conclusion

Again we have seen that the defense of a Reformed charismatic argument is invalid, being either on shaky ground or altogether illusory. Revelation is a glorious book demanding our attention (Rev. 1:3). Nevertheless, caution must be used in its employment. If Paul had some "hard things" to say (2 Pet. 3:16), how much more John in Revelation? And certainly the unity of Scripture will not allow Revelation's employment in a way contradictory to the theology Scripture presents elsewhere.

Conclusion

As we pointed out in the beginning, the whole complex charismatic question is an important contemporary theological and practical issue. There are many factors of the movement which are of interest and which merit close scrutiny. It seems to the present writer that the most crucial issue is the one with which we have been dealing: *the charismatic gift of prophecy*. For this issue impacts directly on the very foundation of our theology: our view of authority, the voice of God speaking in Scripture.

We have attempted to set forth not only a careful orthodox analysis of the phenomenon, but also an unashamedly Reformed one at that. With B. B. Warfield we are convinced that Calvinism is Christianity in its purest expression. In a day when a more broadly based Christianity is in vogue, this might not seem to be wise. Certainly the biggest selling books of our era are not of the Reformed persuasion (excluding those rarities, such as J. I. Packer's, *Knowing God*). Nevertheless, a full-orbed Christianity, such as found in Reformed or Calvinistic theology, will be necessary to counter the theological distortions rampant in the Church today and to draw God's people back to the Word and a worldview based solely on Scripture alone. Reformed theology alone is sufficient to the task. It alone can offer an alternative theology able to call our charismatic brethren back from some of the extremes associated with the charismatic movement.

We have thought it necessary to update and expand our work to incorporate the many fine arguments set forth in a recent evangelical work. That work seeks to establish a mediating position between the standard Reformed view and the popular charismatic one. The book to which we refer is Wayne Grudem's *The Gift of Prophecy In the New Testament and Today*. The issues engaged deserve thoughtful analysis. Consequently, since Grudem's presentation is the most cogent exposition of the question of the New Testament gift of prophecy available, we thought it merited a response.

We are firmly convinced that a sound biblico-theological approach to the whole question, combined with a lexical analysis of the major terms employed and an exegetical study of the crucial passages of Scripture, will lead back to the standard evangelical viewpoint. Recognizing the general truth that the Church needs always to be Reformed and reforming, we remain satisfied with the historic position of evangelical and Reformed thought on this significant issue. It is our prayer that the above presentation might be used to help God's people wrestle with the issues — in a biblical, non-emotional fashion.

Scripture Index

Prepared by Bill Boney

OLD TESTAMENT

Genesis

1:28	134
1:30	134
2:16-17	134
32:30	56

Exodus

4:16	12
7:1	12, 80
33:11	56

Numbers

11:26-29	9
11:29	6
12	9
12:6	6, 21
12:6-8a	37
12:6-8	5, 56
16:25-30	42
16:28-30	63

Deuteronomy

5:4	56
18	3, 8, 43, 64
18:15-22	2, 3, 4
18:15ff	12
18:18ff	63
18:19	4
18:20	4
18:21-22	42, 63
18:22	36
34:10	56

Judges

6:22	56

1 Samuel

9:9	14

Job

12:22	36

Isaiah

2:2-3	71
6	5
46:8-10	36

Jeremiah

1:11-12	5
24:1	5

Ezekiel

1-3	5

8-11	5
20:35	56, 57
37:1-10	5
40-48	5

Daniel

2:19	5, 20
2:22	36
7	5
8	5
10	5
11	5
12	5

Joel

2	7, 8, 9, 17, 36
2:28	5
2:28-29	5
2:28-32	8
3:1	14

Amos

7:1-9	5
8:1-3	5
9:1	5

Micah

4:2-3	71

Zechariah

1:8	5
6:1-8	5

Malachi

4:4	42

NEW TESTAMENT

Matthew

2:6	141
2:20	141
4:8	1
7:11-12	43
7:28-28	106
13:57	19
18	68
18:17	68
18:19	69
21:11	3, 18
21:46	19
23:11	65
23:34	101
23:34-36	141
26:68	106
27:1-7	43
27:42	19
27:45	141
28:18	12
28:19	12

Mark

14:65	106
15:33	141

Luke

1:67	106
4:25	141
7:16	18
11:49	101
13:33	18
21:23	141
22:64	18, 19, 106
24:19	106
24:47	71

John

1:18	54
1:25	3
3:22	141
4:1-6	63
4:19	18, 106
6:14	3, 18
7:40	3, 18
9:17	19
10:35b	1
11:50	49
11:51	105
14:6-9	54
14:17	62
16:13	58
17:17	58
18:29-32	43
19:13-16	43
21:35	132

Acts

1	8
1:1-3	132
1-2	71
1:8	12
1:18	43
1:21-22	54
2	6, 7, 9, 17, 34, 36, 46, 60
2-8	34
2:16-17	8
2:16ff	6
2:17	14, 77
2:17ff	55
2:22-23	43, 141
2:36	141
2:40	132
2:41	34
2:47	34
3:5	99
3:13-15	43, 141
3:21	4
3:22	4
3:24	4
4:4	34
5:30	43
7:37	3
7:52	43, 141
8:29	44, 45
9	34
10-11	56
10:19	45
11	42
11:27	35, 99
11:27-28	36, 50, 88, 106
11:27f	104
11:28	16, 37, 38, 42, 46, 85, 86, 102, 104
11:28b	38
13:1	35, 45, 75, 81, 85, 99, 105, 106
13:1ff	99
13:1-2	22

13:2	44, 45	21:27	68
13:47	12	21:27-31	43
14:25	86	21:27-35	41
15	32, 33, 56	21:31	41
15:7	45	21:35	43
15:9	64	21:32-35	42
15:12	45	21:33	41
15:13	45	22:17ff	105
15:19-20	32	23:9	44
15:22	33, 45	26:6-7	141
15:28	44, 45	27:37	105
15:30-32	33		
15:31	14	**Romans**	
15:32	32, 35, 80, 99, 104, 132	7	39
15:38	39	7:9-11	56
16:6ff	105	9:27-28	141
16:6-7	44	11:25	23
16:9	44	12:1-2	58
16:9f	20	12:6	16, 35, 80, 85, 91, 9, 102, 104, 105, 106, 109, 111, 112
17:11	63, 68	12:6-8	89
18:9	44, 105	12:13	68
19:16	14	13:11-12	141
20:23	44, 45	16:20	141
21	38, 43		
21:4	38, 39, 40, 46, 99	**1 Corinthians**	
21:9	14, 45, 68, 85, 99, 105, 113		
21:10	35, 99, 102		
21:10ff	41, 104	1:2	71
21:10-11	36, 41, 44, 50, 85, 88, 106	1:7	19, 52
		1:12	52
21:11	77, 85	1:14f	14
21:11-12	40	2:4d	20
21:11	45	2:9	53
21:12	45	2:10	19, 20, 21
21:13	42, 45	3:10	
21:14	40, 42	3:12-15	67

3:13	61	12:10	16, 62, 64, 65, 86, 103, 105, 106
4:1	94	12:28	14, 35, 50, 81, 85, 87, 92, 100, 101, 106, 111, 112
4:7	64		
4:17	71	12:28-29	81
4:18-19	67	12:28-30	59
5	68	12:29b	8
5:1	67	12:30b	8
5:4-5	68	12:31	35
5:5	67	13	53, 60
5:9-11	134	13:2	16, 23, 46, 50, 52, 61, 87, 93, 102
5:13	67		
7:7ff	61	13:8	16, 54, 55, 103
7:17	71	13:8-12	93
7:26	141	13:8-13	51
7:29-31	141	13:9	14, 15, 16, 52, 53, 113
8:3	56	13:9-10	55, 57
9:1,2	71	13:10	52
10:12	67	13:10-11	58
11	73	13:11	55, 58
11:2	61	13:12	57
11:4f	16	14	67, 99, 104
11:4,5	15	14:1	14, 15, 16, 92, 100, 103, 105
11:5	72, 73		
11:16	71, 73	14:1ff	99
11:17-19	73	14:2	23, 92
11:20-21	52	14:3	103, 106
11:21-22	73	14:3-5	14, 15
11:28-30	67	14:4	102, 106
11:29	64	14:4f	16
11:33-34	73	14:5	35, 113
12-14	57, 96	14:6	16, 19, 20, 21, 47, 84, 87, 93, 94, 100, 102
12:1-3	46		
12:3	63, 65, 67, 69	14:19-20	55
12:4	46, 69	14:22	16
12:7	46	14:23	67
12:8	86	14:24	14, 15, 92, 103
12:9	46	14:25	103

14:26	19, 20, 21, 52, 93, 94, 96	12:7	20, 94
14:26-30	14	**Galatians**	
14:26ff	96		
14:27	85	1:12	20
14:29	14, 15, 62, 63, 64, 65, 66, 70, 79, 93	2	39
		2:2	20
14:29-30	102	2:13	39
14:29-31	33	2:14	39, 42
14:29-32	47	4:9	56
14:29ff	81		
14:30	19, 20, 21, 81, 87, 93, 103	**Ephesians**	
14:31	14, 15, 106	1:13	62
14:31-32	61	1:17	21, 60, 62
14:32	14, 79, 92	2	32
14:33	52, 70, 71	2:19-22	26
14:34	72, 73	2:20	14, 15, 27, 28, 30, 50, 82, 83, 86, 91, 93, 101, 102
14:36	70, 71	3	59
14:37	14, 15, 70, 115	3:3	20
14:37-38	72	3:4-5	48
14:39	14, 15, 16	3:5	14, 15, 20, 21, 27, 30, 32, 58, 83, 86, 93, 101, 102, 103, 106
13:40	52		
14:24-25	106	3:8-10	27
14:29	68	3:15	93
14:30	84	4:8-12	59
15:12	67	4:11	14, 15, 27, 28, 30, 32, 58, 83, 85, 86, 89, 101, 101, 102, 103, 106, 109, 111, 114
15:31-34	67		
15:33-34	67		
15:51	23, 94		
16:22	67	4:11-12	58, 59
		4:13-14	58
2 Corinthians		4:13-15	59
		5:18	62
11:2-5	67, 71	5:23	23
11:12-15	67		
11:13	72	**Philippians**	
12:1	20	3:2-4	61

3:15	21, 60		
3:19	61	**2 Timothy**	
		1:13	75
Colossians		3:16a	1
		3:16-17	54, 58, 120
3:6	141	4:13	56

1 Thessalonians

Titus

1:7-10	61		
2:2	66	1:9	75
2:2-6	66	1:12	18
2:13	66		
2:14-15	43, 141	**Hebrews**	
2:16	141		
4:1-2	66	1:1-2	54, 128
5	65, 66, 69	3:24	42
5:12	69	5:12-14	120
5:12-13	69	6	56, 61
5:19-20	66	10	56, 61
5:19-21	65	10:25	141
5:20	16, 103	10:37	141
5:20-21	63, 69	13:2	68
5:21	66	13:9	75
5:29-33	69	13:17	69

2 Thessalonians

James

2:2-3	66	1:22	54
2:7	23	1:23-25	56
2:15	5, 66	5:8-9	141
3:1-6	66	5:17	141
3:17	66		

1 Peter

1 Timothy

		1:10	106
5:17	69	1:12	14
5:20	69	2:2	120

4:5	141	7:4-8	141
4:7	141	11	137, 140
5:1-5	69	11:3	14
11:1	49	11:3-13	138
		17	141

2 Peter

		17:5	23
		17:7	23
1:20	75	21	31
2:1	65, 67	21-22	141
3:15-16	49, 56	21:14	31
3:16	142	22:6	14
		22:6-7	141

1 John

		22:7	105
		22:9	14
2:17-18	141	22:10	105
2:18-19	67	22:12	141
4:1	63, 100	22:20	141
4:2-3	65		

3 John

5-8	68

Jude

3	75

Rev

1:1	20, 37, 38, 141
1:3	105, 141, 142
1:7	141
1:20	23
2:20	100
3:10	141
5:5	141
6:10	141
7:1-2	141

www.ingramcontent.com/pod-product-compliance
Lightning Source LLC
Chambersburg PA
CBHW032120090426
42743CB00007B/412